S0-EJQ-048

How Sacraments Celebrate Our Story

Novitiate Library
Mont La Salle
Napa, California

Saint Mary's Press, Christian Brothers Publications, Winona, Minnesota

How Sacraments Celebrate Our Story

Christian Brothers Publications

Mary Perkins Ryan wrote the theological essays for this course. Sheila Moriarty O'Fahey developed the concept for the Journeys Series. She also, along with Sister Maureen Murray, SSND, and Brother Thomas Sullivan, FSC, designed the service units. Stephan Nagel contributed to the orientations and wrote the journal material. Brother Frank Osage, FSC, developed the closing prayers. Jan Van Dyke created the cover artworks.

The development of the Journeys Series has been made possible through a special grant to the Christian Brothers by Mrs. Rose Totino.

Nihil Obstat: David A. Dillon, STD
            Censor Deputatus
Imprimatur: †John R. Roach, DD
            Archbishop of St. Paul and Minneapolis
            July 31, 1978

Third Printing—September 1980

ISBN: 0-88489-104-6
Library of Congress Catalog Card Number: 78-53635

Copyright 1978 by Saint Mary's Press, Terrace Heights, Winona, Minnesota 55987. No part of this text may be reproduced by any means without written permission of the publisher.

Scriptural selections, with the exceptions noted, are from the Revised Standard Version Common Bible, copyright © 1973 by the Division of Christian Education of the National Council of the Churches of Christ in the United States. Used by permission.

Selection from **The Little Prince** by Antoine de Saint-Exupery, translated by Katherine Woods. Copyright © 1943 by Harcourt, Brace and World. Reprinted by permission of Harcourt Brace Jovanovich, Inc. and William Heinemann, Ltd., publishers.

Selection by Emily Dickinson, "I Never Saw a Moor." Published in **Poems by Emily Dickinson**, ed. Martha Dickinson Bianchi and Alfred Leete Hampson. Reprinted by permission of Little, Brown and Company.

Selection from **The Velveteen Rabbit** by Margery Williams. Fourth printing. Reprinted by permission of Doubleday and Company, Inc. and Jean W. Bianco.

Selections from **Working** by Studs Terkel. Copyright © 1972. Reprinted by permission of the author.

Selection from **How Do I Know I'm Doing Right?** by Gerard S. Sloyan, 1976 edition. Copyright © 1976 by the National Office of Confraternity of Christian Doctrine—CCD. Reprinted by permission of the author.

Selection by Elder Olson, "Directions to the Armorer." Copyright © 1959 by the New Yorker Magazine, Inc. Reprinted by permission of The New Yorker.

Selection "All Watched Over by Machines of Loving Grace" excerpted from the book **The Pill Versus the Springhill Mine Disaster** by Richard Brautigan. Copyright © 1968 by Richard Brautigan. Reprinted by permission of Delacorte Press/ Seymour Lawrence.

Selections from "A Bill of Rights," by Norman Perry, OFM, and Tom Schick as published in the July 1970 issue of **St. Anthony Messenger**. Copyright © 1970 by The Franciscan Friars of St. John Baptist Province. Reprinted by permission of St. Anthony Press.

Introduction

Perhaps it is because people tend to see life as a kind of road to be traveled that many of the world's greatest stories are about journeys. One modern journey-story, which has appealed to millions of readers of all ages, is *The Lord of the Rings*, by J.R.R. Tolkien. (Perhaps you know it already. If you don't, you might want to read it.)

The central character, Frodo—a very ordinary person in his own estimation—is entrusted with a most difficult and dangerous mission. He must destroy a Ring which gives unlimited power to its wearer and which tempts him or her to use this power for selfish and destructive purposes. The only way of "unmaking" this Ring is to cast it into the volcanic fires in which it was forged. To do so, Frodo must travel from his quiet home through forests, across rivers, over mountain ranges, and into lands filled with slaves and servants of the Dark Lord who wants to possess the Ring himself so as to enslave the whole world. And throughout his journey, Frodo must resist the temptation to take the Ring, hung on a chain around his neck, and put it on his finger, claiming its power. For to do this would soon destroy him and also make known the Ring's whereabouts to the Dark Lord.

But Frodo did not have to make this difficult journey alone. Eight companions are chosen to go with him, each with a special part to play in achieving his mission and the final victory. And the journey is not all trials and tribulations. The companions meet with sympathizers as well as enemies. And, every so often, they find themselves in friendly places, where they can refresh themselves, tell the tale of their adventures so far and, in celebrating what they have already achieved, renew their hopes of finally accomplishing their mission. These celebrations form an important part of the whole story, for it is most especially on such occasions that the Company of the Ring come to realize how their journey is part of a vast cosmic story which had begun far in the past and which continues into the future.

Probably few of us look forward to adventures like those of Frodo and his companions. Yet most of us do think of our lives as some kind of journey to be taken, with both risky and exciting possibilities. Christian teaching encourages us to use this image. We are members of the "pilgrim Church"—that is, people who believe that they are on a journey with companions both seen and unseen, of all ages and cultures, on their way toward the final realization of the Kingdom of God. And each of us has a vital part to take, however insignificant in our own estimation, in furthering this great and difficult journey of humankind. It is a journey toward the fulfillment of God's promise of "life in all its fullness" (John 10:11) in union with him and one another and the whole cosmos.

In our journeying, we have advantages which the Company of the Ring did not. They had no assurance that their journey would achieve its purpose. But we have God's own assurance that his Kingdom will finally be realized. For Jesus has already made the journey we are now engaged in and so entered into the joy of his Father. In him, the Kingdom is already a reality, although we are still traveling towards it. Still more, he is with us here and now in our journeying, sharing in our difficulties and successes, our sufferings and our joys, and sharing with us his life and his Spirit. As St. Catherine of Siena put it, "All the way to heaven [that is, the Kingdom] is heaven too. For Jesus said, 'I am the Way.'"

On this journey, then, we can enjoy celebrations that are even more refreshing and hope-renewing than those provided for the Company of the Ring. With our Risen Lord, we can celebrate his journey to the Father as giving direction and meaning to our journey. With him, we can celebrate our story as somehow, in spite of our mistakes and failures, carrying on his story—the story of God's journey with humankind, to bring us fully to share his own life. And in so doing, we offer praise and thanks to the Father, with Christ, in his Spirit, looking forward in hope to the final fulfillment of God's promises.

Christians take part in many different kinds of celebrations, and so the first chapter of this course will suggest how any form of genuine celebration can encourage us on our pilgrim way. But our chief and characteristic celebrations are those we call sacraments. Among these the Eucharist is central. For it is "the holy festive meal, in which Christ is received, the memory of his passion is made present, we are filled with God's love and given a pledge of future glory" (St. Thomas Aquinas). In other words, the Eucharist celebrates the whole Christian story, while the other sacraments celebrate different aspects of it.

Unfortunately, we tend to think of the Eucharist and the other sacraments as sacred occasions having very little to do with our ordinary lives, our daily journeying. We need, instead, to try to see these special Christian celebrations, most particularly the Eucharist, as essential events *in* our daily living, our pilgrimage together. Then we can begin to see how taking part in them does give meaning and hope to this pilgrimage. This course is designed to help you explore the sacraments and your own life from this point of view.

Journeys and Journal-Making

Most religion courses about the sacraments use a book someone else has written. But in the Journeys series we want you to create your own resource book—a journal. Although you will have readings from the Scriptures, essays about the sacraments, and prayer sessions as input, the essential material for this course will be the reflections that you yourself record in your journal.

Writing your own course book makes good sense in two ways. First, as was mentioned above, the sacraments celebrate our journey—or pilgrimage—through life. Our journey becomes a deeper, more lasting memory when we use a journal because it helps us become more aware of what we see and think and feel. Even in the few months of this semester, imagine all of the insights, experiences, and memories that will occur to you. Your journal is a tool for preserving these important events in writing and drawing. Looking back on your first journal entries three or four months from now, you will be convinced that this course—and your life—are kinds of journeys.

Second, while you are gaining a fuller understanding of our sacraments, what you learn will be changed by what is uniquely you. *No one else will learn exactly what you will learn in this course,* and your journal will reflect your unique knowledge. Using your journal, you will marvel at what goes on in your mind in the way of accumulated plans, attitudes, ideas, decisions, insights, wishes, opinions, and wisdom. That is why this semester's journey will be unlike a businessman's non-stop flight from Seattle to New York. Rather, it will be a kind of interplanetary voyage or a trailblazing expedition because it is your personal journey, and you are a complex and almost uncharted person.

Why Not Tell Your Story?

To put it another way, the Christian story we celebrate in the sacraments is all about all of us, so there is a place within it for your own story. Like any good story, your story includes characters, story line, themes, and scenery. It might be a delightful, a comic, or sometimes a painful story, but it certainly will contain plenty of action—or changes. In fact, the character or scenery changes sometimes happen so quickly that we lose a sense of our own story for a while, we forget some of the characters, or we don't move on to the next scene when we should.

By trying to describe or explain these life-changes in your journal, you will get a better grasp of your story. You will find better ways of telling it or retelling it so that it makes more sense to you. You may find yourself adding new themes—your hopes, attitudes, wishes—or "writing out" some characters and adding new friends to your story. Of course you can't control all of the events in your life, but your journal helps you to determine how important or unimportant they are to your story. Finally, your journal will give you a chance to fit the events of your story—including those events called sacraments—into the Christian story.

At this point, a word should be said about the journal suggestions you will find in the chapter booklets and in your journal book. They are not intended to limit your journal-making or story-telling. They are merely suggestions. If you think of better ways to tell your story, it is best to do it your way. Remember that your journal should be kept strictly private as a resource book for you alone.

Starting Your Journal

Begin your journal the same way you first dived off a board into a swimming pool: don't think about it very long; just do it. We can all think of any number of reasons not to begin, but they are unimportant. Most of us have never done journal-making before, most of us don't think of ourselves as writers or artists, most of us can't spell or draw really well, and for most of us journal-making doesn't mean much yet . . . but it will.

So loosen up your writing hand and enjoy the feel of pen touching paper. Don't worry anymore about spelling. Don't worry anymore about full and complete sentences. Don't worry if your sketches or charts are somewhat wobbly. Don't worry what anyone is going to think. Just write and draw for the fun of it. Don't forget—a journal is just for you.

Now write your name—big or small, in color or in black ink, perhaps with some kind of decoration. Use a full page of the journal. Add your class or address or date. Now do some or all of the following things. Once you start writing, don't look back. Write very rapidly a statement or two about who you are. Draw a self-portrait in a very simple manner. Draw in enough detail to show where you are. Make a list of the chapters of your life, the nine or ten important events, such as "2. I Became a Scout" or "6. The Family Move to Cleveland." Add anything about yourself that comes to mind. Write something especially nice about yourself. You might write, for instance, "Congratulations, I have begun my journal. Today I have begun to tell my own story."

How These Booklets
Relate to Your Journal-Making

Each new chapter of *How Sacraments Celebrate Our Story* will contain:

1) An *orientation* and reflection to give you some sense of what is to come. In your journal you can jot down any ideas which come from your class discussion.

2) A *reading* which presents the "heart" or message of each chapter. Take time with this reading. Your teacher or some class member can read the essay aloud, pausing at various places to allow you time to think and to talk about the author's ideas. Questions for review and discussion follow each reading.

3) *Journal suggestions* to offer you the chance to record and reflect on the ideas you have collected about the chapter theme and your own life. You will find these suggestions on the back cover of this book. Your journal can be any kind of notebook (e.g., a shorthand notebook or an 8½" x 11" spiral notebook), but it should be one you can carry easily. Use it only for journal entries and not for assignments from other classes.

4) A *service* unit which takes the theme of each chapter and demonstrates how it makes sense in the world at large. This is a planning page with ideas to be worked on individually or as a class.

5) Finally, each chapter concludes with a *closing prayer*. Some members in the class should be assigned to narrate the readings. These readings will require preparation if they are to be effective. The rest of the class should recite the responses together or in groups. This closing prayer might offer gospel readings, a para-liturgy, or scriptural verses which bring together and reinforce the various themes in the chapter.

It's time to begin . . .

What Makes a Celebration?

Chapter 1

1 Orientation

Rituals and Symbols

Words like "rites," "rituals," and "symbols" may have a "churchy" sound to them, but if you reflect on your experience you may discover that they have always been a familiar and common part of your life story. For example, a young child will protest loudly at being abruptly told to leave the warmth and security of the family circle for his or her own dark room unless the family has constructed some appropriate routine to make the passage into night a secure one. Sometimes nothing more is required than that a parent repeat an old story which the child already knows by heart. Then the little one will bury its head in a favorite blanket and drop off to sleep. This blanket (now immortalized by Linus) symbolizes security for the child, and it literally "stands in for" the now absent parent.

Ritual and symbol are important to us all because they offer ways in which we can structure time and space so that certain occasions can be made special, opportunities for celebration. Consider, for example, the complicated ritual of "going to school." For nine months of every year, a school lays out prescribed times and places and courses of study, rituals which are supposed to make it easier for you to learn. Much as students groan about having their days mapped out for them, each summer vacation usually ends with these same people longing for the quiet order of "back to school."

The ritual of going to school generates a host of other rituals and symbols. It also gives rise to all kinds of celebrations. Think of pep rallies for school athletics; meeting with friends at a corner store to "celebrate" the end of a long day; parties to honor the opening night of a school play. Certainly the more involved persons are in the day-to-day workings of their own school, the more they may enjoy and benefit from school celebrations. We say such people have plenty of school spirit.

Perhaps the ultimate celebration of your days in school is graduation itself. Indeed, so elaborate are the happenings and occasions and parties surrounding this time that some teachers of seniors complain that the senior year is nothing but a preparation for these end-of-the-year festivities. And for many students, graduation ceremonies can be happy/sad times, reflecting the fact that many celebrations have a bittersweet flavor.

Rituals, then, are part of our daily lives—in fact, the word simply means "an accustomed way of doing things." Most celebrations need some ritual so that participants will know what they are expected to do next. And rituals usually include the use of symbols—things and actions that mean "more than meets the eye."

The following essay outlines the qualifications you need if you are to take a real part in any kind of celebration, including those special kinds called "sacramental." Before reading this essay, think about some celebrations—at home, at school, with a group, planned and spontaneous—that you have taken part in, and try to list and then discuss the qualities that made them more, or less, successful.

The Little Prince

One of the best discussions of the importance of "rites" comes from a passage in *The Little Prince* by Antoine de Saint-Exupery. The fox is trying to teach the little prince the ways in which they can become friends. While you are reading this excerpt, think of any rituals *you* have for developing friendships. Then discuss these with your classmates.

"What must I do, to tame you?" asked the little prince.

"You must be very patient," replied the fox. "First you will sit down at a little distance from me—like that—in the grass. I shall look at you out of the corner of my eye, and you will say nothing. Words are the source of misunderstandings. But you will sit a little closer to me, every day . . ."

The next day the little prince came back.

"It would have been better to come back at the same hour," said the fox. "If, for example, you come at four o'clock in the afternoon, then at three o'clock I shall begin to be happy. I shall feel happier and happier as the hour advances. At four o'clock, I shall already be worrying and jumping about. I shall show you how happy I am! But if you come at just any time, I shall never know at what hour my heart is to be ready to greet you . . . One must observe the proper rites."

"What is a rite?" asked the little prince.

"Those also are actions too often neglected," said the fox. "They are what make one day different from other days, one hour from other hours. There is a rite, for example, among my hunters. Every Thursday they dance with the village girls. So Thursday is a wonderful day for me! I can take a walk as far as the vineyards. But if the hunters danced at just any time, everyday would be like every other day, and I should never have any vacation at all."

2 Reading and Discussion

What Makes a Celebration?

In the Roman Empire of the fourth century, in a place called Abitene, to take part in the Eucharist was a crime punishable by death. Some Christians who had been arrested for this crime were asked by the judge why they had committed it. "Because," they said, "Christians make the Eucharist and the Eucharist makes Christians. Without the Eucharist we cannot live."

One wonders how many Christians in our country today feel to any degree as those martyrs did. Surely some of us and—who knows—perhaps quite a number do so. But the evidence is all too clear that a great many do not. Many people, both old and young, admit quite openly that they endure each Sunday's Mass from a sense of obligation or loyalty. And many have simply ceased to attend.

This is a sad situation because so many people are missing so much that God wants to give them. Taking part in the Mass and other sacramental celebrations isn't meant to be a routine obligation and a bore. On the contrary, it is meant to help us find life more worthwhile and to help us live more intensely than we would otherwise.

What, then, can we do to "make" the Eucharist and other sacramental celebrations, as those fourth-century martyrs put it, so that they can "make" us more Christian? Most Catholics unfortunately believe that trying to answer this question isn't their business. They think that it is only the business of the Pope and the bishops and liturgy experts to improve the rites, and of parish priests and liturgy committees to improve the carrying-out of the present rites.

The quality of Catholic liturgies is, of course, a primary responsibility of Church authorities and of those people who have a special role in them. But it is also the responsibility of everyone who takes part in these liturgies because they are *celebrations*. (The word "liturgy" in fact originally meant "a public work.") As we all know from our experiences of festive family gatherings and the like, even one person who is out of sorts and can't or won't enter into the spirit of the occasion can spoil it for everyone else. We call such a person a "wet blanket." And this is a very apt expression. For such persons dampen, if they don't succeed in extinguishing, the light and warmth and cheer for our spirits which a celebration should generate. And the more "wet blankets" are present, the more difficult it is for the other participants to get this fire kindled and keep it burning.

Of course, nobody can guarantee the success of a celebration. Among the many different varieties which we have attended, probably only three or four stand out in our memories as having made us feel that life was notably more intense and meaningful than we had suspected. Obviously, much depends on the form and style of the celebration. But these are not our immediate concern here. We are interested, rather, in what is required of participants if they are to help make a celebration rather than wet-blanketing it. What is required is that they be "insiders" both to the spirit of the celebration and to its meaning. And to be such an "insider" calls for certain qualifications in the way of attitudes, knowledge and abilities.

Admittedly, what is done at a Mass or a Baptism or a Confirmation doesn't seem in the least like what you do when you hear some good news and say, "Let's celebrate!" Nor does the ritual of the Mass or of a Baptism seem to have much in common with the ritual of a birthday party or a Thanksgiving dinner. Yet Masses and Baptisms are meant to be celebrations of *the* Good News, of new life and food for the hungry. So if we consider the qualifications needed to be an insider at any kind of celebration, we should begin to see how we could cultivate those needed for sacramental celebrations. And we should also discover how we might more effectively help to "make" any small or large, impromptu or planned celebrations we take part in.

Qualifications for Making Celebrations

The absolutely indispensable requirement already mentioned is that you really want to take part. A celebration of Grandmother's eightieth birthday will be a very dismal affair if most of her family would much rather be watching a game on TV.

But why do people want to celebrate? Because they are so happy about some event that they feel a need to get together with other people who are also happy about it, and to re-present it in some way which will increase their happiness in it and the hope that it gives to their lives. Suppose, for instance, that a friend of yours gets a much-needed job. He naturally wants to celebrate with some people who know him well and will be happy about this event with him and for him. He invites you to a party to have some drinks and a festive meal. While you are eating and drinking, you re-present your friend's job-getting in your conversation, talking about how he got it, what it means to him, his prospects for the future. And you also re-present the common happiness of the group over this event by drinking a toast to your friend's good fortune before sharing a meal. So you and the others each help to make this occasion, both by what you say and what you do. And it in turn makes each of you feel happier over your friend's good fortune than you would have otherwise,

and also more hopeful about your own future. Like every celebration that really "works," it makes you feel that if this good thing *has* happened, then other good things *will* happen.

What, then, are the qualifications needed to be an insider at such a celebration or any other? First, you need to be familiar with the event being celebrated and, even more important, with the story of which it is a part. The more familiar you are with your friend's life-story, for instance (and so understand more fully what getting the job means to him), the more celebrating this event will mean to you. Or again, at a birthday party, you don't need to know much about the details of the person's birth—just that it happened. But the better you know the life-story of the person whose birthday it is, the more the fact that he or she is alive and well after so many years may be a cause of happiness and hope to you.

But you also need to feel that this story has in some way affected your story for the better— that it is in some sense *your* story and you are glad that it is. If you go to the birthday party of someone who had caused you and other people deep unhappiness, you hardly feel like celebrating his or her story, even though it has been bound up with your own. In the same way, a Chinese or a Swede can only be a polite outsider at a Thanksgiving celebration since the history of the United States isn't their history. Citizens of the United States who feel that their parents or grandparents were badly mistreated by the descendants of the Pilgrims may not feel that they are "into" the Thanksgiving mood either.

In other words, to be an insider at a celebration you have to be within a community of persons united by their delighted identification with a particular story. The fans of a winning team, for example, are all happy to be identified with its history, and so they can, so to speak, pool and increase their delight in its victory even if they don't know one another's names. For the moment, at least, they form a community and are glad that they do so.

But you also need to be "inside" the way in which the community re-presents the event being celebrated. That is, you need to be able to sense and respond to the meanings which the actions carrying out the celebration, and the persons and things involved, are intended to convey. At a birthday party, for instance, you need to sense what the cake with its lighted candles—one for each year of the person's life and "one to grow on"—and the ritual of carrying it in, blowing out the candles, wishing, cutting and sharing the cake, are all "saying."

The Language of Symbols

This is the language of the kind of signs called "symbolic." These are not the kind of signs which border our highways representing the shape of the road ahead by a curved arrow or a squiggle, or telling you about the next exit or the legal speed limit. Such signs only give you information, and very specific information. Symbolic signs, however, convey many levels of meaning, not only to our minds but to our whole body-spirit selves. The candles on a birthday cake can tell you much more than how old the person is. Lights shining in darkness "speak" to human beings about knowing what they are doing and where they are going, about hope and truth. Again, sharing food and drink is an action that "speaks" to people of all cultures about sharing life. Thus the birthday party ritual represents a person's story as in some way light-giving and life-sharing. And so it can make the participants feel happier about their own lives and more hopeful about acting as light-givers and life-sharers.

Of course, people at birthday parties don't engage in such an analysis of what they are doing and what it is doing to them. The birthday-cake ritual presumably "speaks for itself." But the participants are affected to the degree to which they are sensitive to the meanings of lighted candles and shared food. These symbols might be called "natural" since they are based on the way we are made: we need light to see and food to live. Yet people who have never been deprived of light or food tend to be less sensitive to their meanings than people who live without electricity and on the verge of starvation. And so we may well need to re-sensitize ourselves to these basic natural symbols.

Other symbols gain their meanings from the particular ways in which people in a given culture think and feel about the realities they experience. In our culture, we try to emphasize the importance of individual persons, and we tend to over-emphasize the importance of a person's age. So it seems "natural" to us to celebrate birthdays. But a person brought up in another culture without these emphases would find it hard to get inside our feelings about them.

On the other hand, we can cultivate our sensitivity to these "more than meets the eye" meanings of things and persons and actions. We can do so by reflection, by using our imaginations, and by paying attention to what persons and things and actions might have to "say" beyond that which is immediately obvious. And the more we do so, the richer and more interesting our lives will become.

To summarize the requirements we have mentioned for being an insider at a celebration—they are: (1) to want to take part in it because (2) you are familiar with its story and (3) feel that it is in some way your story, and that it has made your story a better and happier one, and (4) because you feel united with the other people who feel the same way about the story, and (5) you are sensitive to the meanings of the actions re-presenting the story and the persons and things involved in them. Taking part in the celebration increases your happiness and hopefulness.

These requirements include knowledge, attitudes, and abilities, and we can cultivate all three so as to become more and more insiders at one or another kind of celebration. We can, then, do so for sacramental celebrations. They celebrate the greatest story of all, the story of God's presence and action in human life and history, and we can always become more familiar with this story. We can always realize more deeply that it is our story, the story that gives our lives meaning and hope. We can always make it more fully our story by more consciously and fully trying to take our part in it day after day. And we can always grow in sensitivity to the ways in which sacramental celebrations re-present the story.

As was mentioned earlier, every genuine cele-

bration declares in its own way: since this good thing which we are celebrating *has* happened, then other good things can happen, in spite of the destruction and waste and misery so evident in our world. And so it is worthwhile trying to make more good things happen, even though we are so often frustrated and fail in our efforts. This is why we need genuine celebrations of all kinds—why, in a very real sense, we cannot live without them. For unless we feel—at least occasionally—that our lives have some meaning and are good, we feel that we might as well be dead.

This is why it is worthwhile trying to increase the different kinds of knowledge, attitudes, and abilities which enable us to help "make" genuine celebrations of many kinds and to be "made" by them. And this is why it is supremely worthwhile to keep fitting ourselves to help "make" sacramental celebrations. For they can reassure us that our trust in the goodness of Ultimate Reality is based on what God has done and is doing in human history, in our history. They can "tell" us, beyond what words can convey, about the meaning and hope God gives our lives.

In these essays, then, we will explore some ways of becoming more fully "insiders" to sacramental celebrations. We will first consider becoming familiar with the Christian story so as to see it both as God's story and our own. (I hope that it is clear how we are using the word "story," not in the sense in which an English teacher tells a student, "That's a good story you've written," but in the sense in which you eagerly ask, "What's the story?" when you come home and find that something important has happened which you don't know about.)

Then we will reflect on ways in which the Christian story fits our human experience while giving it new and undreamed-of dimensions, and go on to discuss the kinds of attitudes and actions called for if we are trying to live it as our own story.

Questions for Review:

1) Who is responsible for the quality of liturgies?

2) To help make a liturgy a real celebration you need to be an "insider." How would you describe an "insider"?

3) According to the author of this essay, what is symbolic language?

4) What usually happens when we train (cultivate) our sensitivity to the "more than meets the eye" meanings of things and persons and actions?

5) What do sacramental celebrations really celebrate?

6) How does the writer of this essay want us to understand the word "story"?

7) Why do we need genuine celebrations of all kinds?

Questions for Discussion:

1) What is the difference between attending a play or a movie and attending a celebration?

2) Have you ever felt like an "outsider" at a celebration? Why? Discuss and compare with others' experiences.

3) Advertising relies on symbols to persuade people to buy products. What are some of these symbols? Do you allow them to influence you? Should you allow them to do so?

4) What are some of the symbols in your parish church? Do they "say" anything to you? What do you think they might have said to the people who chose them and put them there?

3 Journal Suggestions

Until now you may not have thought of our liturgies as celebrations. In fact, there are many celebrations in our lives which we take more or less for granted. The suggestions given on the back cover of this book will give you an opportunity to become more conscious of celebrations and more able to participate in them.

4 From Sacrament to Service

We use the word "service" both for "any religious ceremony, usually public worship" and for "work done or duty performed for another or others" (Webster's New World Dictionary). One of the purposes of this course is to bring out the inter-relationship between these two kinds of "service"— that trying to serve others' needs lovingly and skillfully is both the prerequisite and the effect of taking part in sacramental "services."

The essays indicate the general lines of service to others proposed and celebrated in the Eucharist and in the other sacraments. The service sections, then, offer opportunities to explore some of the qualities and varieties of service.

The essay in the first chapter brought out some of the requirements for being an "insider" at a celebration of any kind. Now you are going to engage in an experience designed to help you realize the importance of becoming an "insider" to the feelings of the people you are trying to serve. Consider the following story.

A Catholic high school decided that for a Christmas project, each class would put together a basket of food and deliver it personally to a poor family in the neighborhood. The sophomore class was particularly enthusiastic about this chance to show their concern for people in need. They worked hard to make their basket a fine one, collecting not only basic foods but interesting delicacies and delights to make the family's Christmas a happy occasion.

On the appointed day, representatives from the class brought their gift to the family located for them by the Catholic Social Services. When the mother of the household came to the door, they explained their class project and offered her the basket. To their amazement, the woman looked at the group, said nothing, and then shut the door.

At first the class was incensed at what they felt was rude and ungrateful behavior. But after tempers cooled, they began to rethink the situation. Most especially, they tried to see what had happened from the woman's point of view.

Imagine that something like this happened to your class. What might be your reactions? Can you think of any good explanation for what the woman did? Can you think of some things that a class might do to help poor families that might be more effective than the actions of this class?

5 Closing Prayer

Theme:

Moments to Celebrate

Opening Song:

"A Time for Building Bridges" by Rev. Carey Landry or "Turn, Turn, Turn" by Pete Seeger.

Opening Prayer:

Lord Jesus, we sometimes rush around each day expecting "big miracles" and tend to overlook the little things that happen each day. Lord, thank you for all the little things that make each day "special" and something worth celebrating and living each moment to the fullest. Amen.

First Reading:

Read the excerpt from the book *The Little Prince* by Antoine de Saint-Exupery on page 10.

Reflection:

Share an experience in your life when you really had something to celebrate.

Second Reading:

(Create a slide/music presentation or read the following excerpt.)

A reading from the book of Ecclesiastes.

For everything there is a season, and a time for every matter under heaven: a time to be born, and a time to die; a time to plant, and a time to pluck up what is planted; a time to kill, and a time to heal; a time to break down, and a time to build up; a time to weep, and a time to laugh; a time to mourn, and a time to dance; a time to cast away stones, and a time to gather stones together; a time to embrace, and a time to refrain from embracing; a time to seek, and a time to lose; a time to keep, and a time to cast away; a time to rend, and a time to sew; a time to keep silence, and a time to speak; a time to love, and a time to hate; a time for war, and a time for peace (3:1-8).

Giving Thanks:

Right Side: Thank you, Lord, for my family, friends, and relatives.
Left Side: We thank you, Lord.
Right Side: Thank you, Lord, for the happy moments in my life.
Left Side: We thank you, Lord.
Right Side: Thank you, Lord, for all the ways in which you help us.
Left Side: We thank you, Lord.
(Additional prayers may be added at this time.)

Closing Prayer:

Father, we give you thanks for each moment of our life. We give you thanks for those special times that we celebrate—birth, birthdays, anniversaries, and graduations. Amen.

Closing Song:

"Song of Thanksgiving" by Monks of Weston Priory.

Becoming Familiar with the Story

Chapter 2

1 Orientation

In the sixteenth century, the Italian missionary Matteo Ricci brought with him to China a map of the world showing the new discoveries in America. The Chinese were glad to learn about America, but one thing about the map displeased them. The Chinese had always regarded themselves as the Middle Kingdom, that is, the kingdom at the center of things. But Ricci's map divided the earth down through the Pacific Ocean, thus placing China on the extreme righthand edge. To satisfy his friends, Ricci redrew the map, splitting the Atlantic instead, so that China appeared to be in a more central place. To this day, maps are commonly drawn this way in that part of the world.

What this incident illustrates is that there are often several ways of telling the same story, depending on your particular point of view. Nowhere is this more true than when we are trying to piece together the various elements of our own *family* story. Before we can even remember, our parents were already relating to us tales and adventures of our forebears. Perhaps Great-uncle Luke was a captain who sailed the Great Lakes, or Cousin Emma could trace her ances-try back to the Mayflower, or Grandfather Kelly left Ireland because the British "had a price on his head." All these stories, woven together, lent us a sense of pride in our own specialness. We became conscious of the uniqueness of our family name.

When we began school and met others of different family names, we were gradually introduced to new stories, those of the region of the country we lived in. If we grew up in Southern California, we probably learned that Spanish missionaries were the first to introduce Western ways to the New World. If we lived in New England, we thought of the Pilgrims as our founding fathers and mothers. The region of the country we lived in determined in large measure who our saints and folk heroes were. Whether we and our classmates liked Paul Bunyan or Paul Revere, Kateri Tekakwitha or Our Lady of Guadalupe, Thomas Jefferson or Jefferson Davis, depended as much on our perceptions of geography as of history. Our family story became part of a widening circle of stories that helped shape our regional and, eventually, our national identity.

Just as those around us handed on to us a particular cultural and national identity, so they were anxious that we should also inherit a rich religious tradition. The stories they told us were meant to help us in our own efforts to give a shape and direction to our lives. But at some stage in our development, we have to make some decisions as to which stories we want to live by. And it is especially important that we try to discover what the Christian story means to us. Whatever versions we have heard of it have come down to us through the life stories of other people. Before we can accept these, we need to try to hear the story anew . . . just as if we were listening to it for the first time. Part of the purpose of the following reading is to help you do just this.

Share with your classmates your reflections on the following questions: Do you remember how you first heard about the Christian story? From whom and when? Was it in response to some question you had? Or was someone trying to explain a certain symbol or feast day? In coming to understand your religious tradition, who do you consider to have been your best storytellers? What most impressed you about their version of the story?

2 Reading and Discussion

Becoming Familiar with the Story

As we saw in the previous chapter, to help "make" a celebration, we need to know the story behind it, and the more familiar we are with it the better. How familiar are we, then, with the Christian story as both God's story and our own?

Probably most of us began to hear about Jesus when we were very little. As we grew older, we picked up bits and pieces of the Christian story, and our parents and religion teachers tried to give us some idea of the main outline and message of the story and how it concerns us. In our culture, almost everyone learns something about the Christian story. But to people who aren't Christians, it is just a story. They don't think that it has anything to do with them. We learned about it as the story that gives meaning and shape to our lives.

Obviously, we have learned it as being our story because those who brought us up belong to the community of people who accept the Christian story as God's story of what human life is all about. We were formally admitted to this community when we were baptized into it as babies. But as we grow up, we have to begin to consider whether we want to live as active members, freely accepting the Christian story as our story and consciously taking part in it. Nor can this be a once-for-all decision. We have to make it again and again all our lives long.

To accept the Christian story as God's story we need the gift of faith, a gift which God will certainly keep on giving us if we ask him. But to make any kind of a real decision, we also need to become more and more familiar with this story as we grow and change and meet new situations. Many people, unfortunately, think that what they learned about it as children and what they then understood it to mean is all there is to it. They don't see any reason for re-examining it because they are convinced that they have heard it all before.

This is a great mistake, for several reasons. In the first place, since it is God's story about how he has acted and is acting and will act in human history—in our history—its wealth of meaning for us must be as inexhaustible as he is. We can never know other human persons so well that we couldn't know them better, that they can't surprise us. How much more so with our knowing God and knowing about him . . .

Then also, you don't see and feel about things now as you did when you were younger. So you couldn't have been told the story when you were a child in a way that would be adequate to your present way of experiencing life and trying to deal with it. As we grow and change, however old we are, we need to keep hearing and reflecting on the many ways in which Christians have been telling the story through the centuries and are telling it today.

This is the reason for the Liturgy of the Word in the Mass: to give us different parts and aspects of the story in the words of Scripture, and in the homilist's attempt to bring out some of its meaning to our Christian community. This is also the reason for religion classes and study-groups and all the various methods Christians use to help themselves and one another explore the story's infinite wealth of meaning.

Further, the Christian story has been told and retold over thousands of years by people of many different cultures, in many different situations, asking different questions about life, and telling the story to different audiences for different purposes. The Scriptures, we believe, are the standard by which to judge whether a given "telling" is faithful to the story. But the Scriptures themselves were written over many centuries, from many different viewpoints, in many different literary forms. Even the four gospels tell the story with different emphases, for different original audiences, and for different purposes. So we may safely conclude that God wants the story told in many different ways, both because of its inexhaustible wealth of meaning and because it is to be told to human persons with different world outlooks and experiences.

Theologians are people particularly trained for the task of discovering what the story has to say to new situations, what light new discoveries and events and realizations shed on versions of the story current in their communities, and how to express the story in ways at once faithful to the Scriptures and meaningful to people here and now. But we all have a part to take in this process as we try to find out what the story says to us.

Since we are members of the Catholic Christian community, we expect the Pope and our bishops to give us guidance as to how to interpret the story. And we believe that God's own Spirit is with the Christian community in such a way that, in spite of human limitations and failings, it somehow keeps on telling the story, and finding new or forgotten meanings in it in response to new questions.

The Story and Today's Questions

We can see this process of discovery and rediscovery continuing in our own times. For several centuries in Western culture, people generally were convinced that things were getting better and better with the advance of human knowledge and technology. In the United States, people also believed that even if they themselves were not prospering, their children would have a chance to do so. But the first of these beliefs now seems to be contradicted by the stark realization that the resources of our planet are limited, and that increased knowledge and more advanced technology seem to be creating greater and more complex problems for humankind. And the second belief now seems to be equally unfounded. While the rich get richer and more powerful, the poor and the middle-class increasingly find themselves trapped in no-win situations, with very little hope that things will be better for their children.

More and more people, then, are feeling that life is too difficult and are asking "What's the use?" Why not turn to drink or drugs or sex or passive TV-watching or whatever might provide some momentary comfort? God, if there is a God, must be incompetent and uncaring.

Now this would certainly be true if the God of Christian belief were a God "up there," managing human affairs from afar—a God outside of as well as above the human situation. And, unfortunately, all too many people think that this is the kind of God Christians are supposed to believe in.

Happily, Scripture scholars and theologians and "ordinary" Christians have been taking a new look at the Christian story and realizing that a God like this is not the God revealed in the Scriptures and the main lines of Christian tradition.

Our God is most intimately and intensely both with and for human beings. The Bible does, indeed, often picture him as "enthroned above." But this, and images like it, are meant to convey something of his complete "Otherness." Perhaps human beings tend to locate their God or gods "up there" because until recently we couldn't go very far up, and locating God where we couldn't go seemed a good way to express "Otherness." Yet God's "Otherness," as modern philosophers and theologians are rediscovering, doesn't mean distance, but rather utter nearness. God is "closer to us than we are to ourselves." "In him we live and move and have our being" (Acts 17:28).

Thus "Our Father who art in heaven" does not mean that the Ultimate Source and Goal of our being is located in some distant corner of the universe, much less outside it. It means that he is related to us as our Father in some absolute, glorious, and loving way which our best dreams of what parents might be like can only dimly reflect.

So also with the phrase in the Creed that Jesus "ascended into heaven." It doesn't mean that he went off somewhere in space. It means that as man he is now living the very life of God,

20

The Heart of the Christian Story

The central event in the story as told in the Hebrew Scriptures is about the LORD's freeing the Hebrews from painful and degrading slavery in Egypt, making an agreement with them to "walk in his ways," and bringing them through many dangers to the Promised Land. This is the basic biblical story line—the LORD frees people *from* deadly situations, *for* a new and better life which they must freely choose and pursue. It is repeated over and over in the history of individuals and of the whole people. Poets sing this story, and wise men reflect on it. The prophets recall it to persuade the people to repent and return to the LORD's life-giving ways. For when they wander from his paths of justice, mercy, and love, they find themselves once again in desperate situations. But when they repent, God again rescues them.

This story, first sketched in the events of the Exodus, is a continuing story, and it is one with the promise of a final happy ending. Because the LORD has freed his people and given them new life in the past, he will do so again. He has been faithful to his covenant even when they have not, and he will still be faithful. In the end, his love will change their "stony hearts" to "hearts of flesh" and enable them to achieve fullness of life in what the Bible calls the "Reign" or "Kingdom" of God.

So Jewish people throughout the centuries have been celebrating these great deeds of the LORD, as if they had happened to them personally. The story of the Exodus is their story, shedding light on their present and future, however dark these may seem.

The life, death, and glorification of Jesus are seen in the New Testament, not only as continuing this same story but as revealing new depths of God's love for all persons and giving us assurance of its final victory. Jesus proclaimed

so that he can be with us with the loving nearness of God. In this same way, he will "come again" in some new realization of that nearness.

And when we pray, "Come, Holy Spirit," this doesn't mean that we expect him to come where he wasn't already present. God is always offering us his Spirit, to enable us to love him and one another with his own love. When we ask the Spirit to "come," we are opening ourselves to this enabling.

Thus God makes himself most intimately present to human persons. But we have to want to be present to him. As communication between two people is a two-way process, so with us and God. He will not force us to love as he does. He can only invite us. He invites us because he loves us and wants us to share the infinite riches of his life and to share that life as whole persons in community with one another and with him. The Christian story, then, is the story of God's involvement with human persons to invite and enable them to achieve the life in abundance which he wants for us.

that the Kingdom of God is at hand and urged people to change their ways to God's ways so as to prepare for it. Through his teaching and his actions, he showed afresh what these ways are—to free people from diseases of the body, mind, and spirit, to welcome outcasts, to forgive again and again, to give extravagantly, to serve one another's needs lovingly, even to lay down one's life. He said that, in all this, he was doing what God had given him to do—the God of Israel whom he called "Father," even using the familiar endearing term rather than the formal one. And he invited his followers to enter into the same intimate relationship and so to be able to act as God's dear children.

Then he himself went through his "Exodus," his death on the cross, in loving trust in his Father's love and life-giving power. And the Father raised him to a new life, free from all the limitations of human life as we know it, completely "inspirited" by God's spirit. His disciples experienced him as living this new kind of life and "pouring out" this Spirit upon them so that they could do, as he had promised, even greater things than he had done.

In Jesus, the Kingdom of God is already a reality. But the story is still continuing and will continue until the victory of God's love is fully achieved. And it will be achieved by people turning to God's ways, acting to free themselves and others from everything that prevents them from loving and acting lovingly, helping one another to the "life in all its intensity" that God wishes for every human person. Thus all the actions we take along these lines do matter—even when they don't seem to be accomplishing anything. For since we are empowered by God's spirit, we share in the hidden effectiveness of his love which is already victorious in Jesus.

Certainly this is not the effectiveness we would expect from an expert in "human engineering." Its results are not at all evident. People keep on acting against their own best interests. They keep on acting selfishly and cutting themselves off from others. But perhaps it is something like the effectiveness of a wise and patient teacher or parent, who respects the freedom and uniqueness of persons and helps them grow and mature as free persons with the love that encourages but does not force this growth.

Nor does the Christian story offer a pat answer to the problem of human suffering. It only tells us that God is with all human persons in their suffering. He somehow suffers with them. In Jesus, God has entered our human situation and has suffered as we do.

This is at least one reason why the Christian story is to be proclaimed to "the whole creation" (Mark 16:15) and why telling it so as to bring out God's "nearness" is so important. Christians are, at long last, beginning to realize that the Jewish people remain God's Chosen, with a special mission to accomplish in human history. We are also beginning to realize more clearly that God has and does reveal himself in many ways to people of all cultures and religions and that we have much to learn from them about him and his relationships with humankind. We recognize that God offers his self-communication, his Spirit, to every human person, and that those who accept this gift are helping to prepare for the Reign of God and will share in that Reign.

But the Christian Church and its members still have the commission to proclaim, through their words and actions and celebrations, the love of God and his will for human well-being uniquely manifested in Jesus Christ. For they can act and celebrate in the unique assurance and hope given by trusting faith in this love—the assurance that human actions and sufferings do matter, that the Reign of God will come and will be at once God's work and ours, in which we will rejoice with his joy.

Questions for Review:

1) Why do we need to become more and more familiar with God's story?

2) What is the reason for the Liturgy of the Word in the Mass?

3) What can we conclude from the fact that the gospels were written over many centuries, from many different viewpoints, and in many literary forms?

4) What are some of the tasks a theologian is trained to do?

5) How do modern philosophers and theologians explain God's "otherness"?

6) What is the central event of the story as told in the Hebrew Scriptures?

Questions for Discussion:

1) We all find ourselves acting like "different persons" with different people—members of our family, friends, etc. Does this mean that we don't have any real "I"—or that different people in different situations call out different aspects of our "I"?

2) In the Psalms, God is compared to a fortress, a rock, a refuge, a king, a shepherd, a gracious host . . . In Jesus' parables, to a father, a farmer sowing seed, the owner of a vineyard, a rich man entrusting his servants with his money, a woman looking for a lost coin . . . Why do you think that the Scriptures use so many and varied comparisons? Which of those you are familiar with do you find most helpful? How?

3) In the light of the essay you have just read, how would you answer the question: Why be a Christian?

3 Journal Suggestions

History books have concentrated on the stories of the so-called great people of the past—Napoleon, George Washington, Abraham Lincoln, and others like them. Perhaps even your own family history is colored by this tendency to glorify some persons and to forget others. Use your journal to investigate your personal history, following suggestions you will find for this chapter on the back cover of this book.

4 From Sacrament to Service

Just as there are several ways of understanding the Christian story, so too there are different approaches towards living a life of Christian service. Sometimes "loving our neighbor" literally means extending a helping hand to a particular person in need. At other times, it may require that we work to correct those injustices in the social, economic, or political systems that *cause* people to suffer. In his own life, action, and teaching, Jesus exemplified the many ways by which we can care for others and how we can change institutions which oppress people and which make them into "outsiders."

Like Jesus, we can show concern for others in different ways. For example, we can assist persons in need on a *one-to-one* basis. We can also serve people's needs by uniting in *group or community* efforts. And we can try most effectively by group efforts—to correct injustices by working to change those institutions that perpetuate them. All these ways are valuable and necessary. How we choose to act and at what level will be determined partly by our own personality and temperament and partly by the way we perceive what is needed in a situation.

Suppose that a person, confined to a wheelchair with cerebral palsy, wants to attend your school but cannot because of the number of steps outside each entryway. If you wanted to help this person, you might do several things. You could get some of your classmates to volunteer to carry him or her up and down the stairs each day. Or you could try to persuade the administration in the school to put ramps in at all the accesses so that any person with a similar disability could come to your school. What would be the consequences of each action? In the first case, you might form a close friendship with the person you assisted and, at the same time, gain a better understanding of what it means to be disabled. In the second case, there might be a long-range satisfaction in knowing that you succeeded in helping persons to help themselves and that you were able to sensitize the administration to the special needs of the handicapped. Take a few minutes to think about this situation. Which course of action personally appeals to you more? What action do you think might appeal to the person with the disability?

Since most of us are more experienced with helping people in a one-to-one relationship, this course of studies will concentrate particularly on the kinds of community, political, and social involvements that are often more difficult but which may, in the long run, effect more permanent changes for a greater number of people.

5 Closing Prayer

Theme:

Our Story as Christian People on Our Journey . . .

Opening Song:

"All the Earth Proclaim the Lord"

Leader:

"Yahweh called me, before I was born, from my mother's womb, he pronounced my name" (Isaiah 49:1). Our story began with our parents; we have been called to begin our lifelong journey to grow as God's people.

First Story:

Read the story or show the film *The Giving Tree* by Shel Silverstein.

Reflection:

Take time to think about these questions:

1) Do the earlier pleasures differ from the things the boy wants from the tree as he grows older?

2) How does their relationship change as the boy grows older?

3) What can you give to others besides things? How is this kind of giving part of Jesus' message?

Second Story:

Let us listen to a story about Jesus and his mission, a reading from the Acts of the Apostles.

But Peter, standing with the eleven, lifted up his voice and addressed them, "Men of Judea and all who dwell in Jerusalem, let this be known to you, and give ear to my words" (2:14).

"Men of Israel, hear these words: Jesus of Nazareth, a man attested to you by God with mighty works and wonders and signs which God did through him in your midst, as you yourselves know—this Jesus, delivered up according to the definite plan and foreknowledge of God, you crucified and killed by the hands of lawless men" (2:22-23).

"This Jesus God raised up, and of that we all are witnesses. Being therefore exalted at the right hand of God, and having received from the Father the promise of the Holy Spirit, he had poured out this which you see and hear" (2:32-33).

Our Response to Our Story:

Right Side: Lord, help us to reach out to others in need.

Left Side: Help us, Lord, be people who care and who believe your story.

Right Side: Lord, help us to accept graciously what others have to offer us.

Left Side: Help us, Lord, be people who care and who believe your story.

Right Side: Lord, help us to love in deed and in truth.

Left Side: Help us, Lord, be people who care and who believe your story.

(Additional prayers may be added at this time.)

Closing Song:

"Listen" by Monks of Weston Priory.

The Christian Story and the Human Story

Chapter 3

1 Orientation

I never saw a moor,
  I never saw a sea;
Yet know I how the heather looks,
  And what a wave must be.

I never looked on God,
  Nor visited in heaven;
Yet certain am I of the spot
  As if a chart were given.

Where do we look for God? Emily Dickinson, the author of this poem, writes from the firm conviction that, although she has never seen God, he does in fact exist. The following essay will point out many reasons why believing in God makes sense. Some of these reasons may be familiar to you; others may not. But before you consider them, it is important to search your own experience for possible traces of his presence.

Was there ever a time when you had a glimpse of what it might be like to "visit in heaven"? One young sophomore described her exhilaration at the moment when she succeeded in surfboard riding. As she stood up on the board, she said she was emotionally "carried out of herself." While riding the crests, she felt overwhelmed by a sense of awe in the power of all crea-

tion. A young man told of a time when he and a friend had a long and wonderful conversation. "We could have talked together all night," he said. "Neither of us wanted the evening to end." These situations and others like them give us hints and intimations that there is a Reality in our midst who transcends time and space. This Reality whom we name God calls to us from the depths of our human experience. In times of delight, surprise, wonder, and joy, he seems especially present.

But he is no less present in those situations which test the limits of our courage and hope. Sometimes suffering can force us to look beyond the limitations and the seeming futility of a situation to seek help from another. And in thus reaching out, we come to feel we are supported. This very ability to trust in someone beyond ourselves can be a sign of God's ultimate care for us and of his everlasting fidelity. Whenever work or play, pain or delight, push us to question the limits of our own existence, we can become more conscious of the "Beyond in our midst" whose presence in our life makes all reality "gracious."

If our own experiences provide us with the first clues by which we recognize God's reality, how do we separate what is human from what is divine? Is God just a glow of satisfaction after a good meal? Or an aspirin tablet for life's headaches? Is he a giant security blanket by which we can hide from trouble? Surely not. God *is* hidden in the events of everyday life. But it is only when we allow these events to open out for us a transforming vision of life and of living that we sense we are "in touch" with God.

Becoming aware of God's presence often means becoming more attentive to the transforming quality of some of our own experiences. Read the following list of descriptive words and see if any of these evoke memories of some occasion in which you have had this sense of "going beyond" and returning somehow changed. Describe this occasion to your classmates or in your journal. Did the experience help you to remain open to something beyond yourself?

Delight	Fear	Pain
Wonder	Peace	Trust
Awe		

2 Reading and Discussion

The Christian Story and the Human Story

Some years ago, I was talking with two young women, graduates of Catholic high schools, who were then juniors at Smith College. I asked them what they had found most difficult about their first months as freshmen. They both said immediately, "The absence of God." I asked, "Like how?" and they answered, "Oh, you know

. . . at school there was the chapel and the Sisters' habits and holy pictures on the walls and prayers before class. But, of course, there's nothing like that here."

Whether you go on to college or to the world of jobs and job-seeking, you will probably find yourself in this same kind of situation. You may well be working and talking and playing with people who don't share your belief in God's gracious presence or in his loving involvement in human history. There may not be any obvious reminders of the Christian story around to help you. This doesn't mean, of course, that God is "absent." Wherever we are, he is closer to us than we are to ourselves. It does mean that you will need to make some positive efforts to find other people with whom to learn more about the Christian story, to try to live it, and to celebrate it. And celebrations are particularly important since, by taking part in them, we bring our daily experiences into the light and warmth of the Christian community's living re-presentation of its story.

Such efforts are, perhaps, needed even more today than when I had that conversation with the two young women. Now many more people seem to be interested in the Beyond in the midst of human life than were ten years ago. Campuses and parks are filled to overflowing with very vocal proponents of many kinds of religions. On TV programs we are exhorted to "accept Christ as our personal Savior," and public figures openly profess that they have been "born again" through an experience of Christ's love.

It is, perhaps, less difficult to live as a Catholic Christian believer in a situation where God is politely ignored than to do so in one where he is presented in so many guises, some attractive and some offensively bizarre or sentimental. We should, indeed, as part of our education for living in a pluralist society, learn something about Christian traditions other than our own, and something about the other great world religions, and look for the light they may shed on our own version of the Christian story. But to do this and get anything out of it other than bewilderment, we need to make and to keep

making the efforts mentioned above. For then we will be doing our part in cultivating the gift of faith.

Basically, faith might be defined as the ability to recognize that there is a gracious Beyond in the midst of human life. Notice that the Creed has us say, "I believe *in* God . . ." When you tell other persons, "I believe in you" or "I have faith in you," you mean much more than that you believe that these people really exist. You mean that you trust them, that you have confidence in what they will say and do. And so with faith *in* God. It implies the gift of hope that, in spite of the way things look, in the end "all shall be well, and all shall be well, and you shall see it yourself that all manner of things shall be well" (Julian of Norwich).

For Christians, this basic faith and hope are affirmed and given shape and substance by the Christian story of God's loving involvement in human history in and through Jesus Christ and his Spirit. It is easy, then, to see why faith and hope in God must be his gift. Only his Spirit can enable us to know and trust in the Source of our being and all beings. And it is only through his Spirit that we are able to hope that, in the end, love and life will win over divisiveness and death.

God will go on giving us these abilities as long as we do not refuse them, and he will give us these abilities more fully as we try to cultivate them. But these gifts are meant to take root, so to speak, in our ordinary human capacities to understand and reason, to imagine and to wonder. So we should always be ready and able to give a *reason* for our hope (1 Pet. 3:15). That is, we should be able to explain on grounds which people can grasp why it is not *un*reasonable to believe in God and how it is possible to see the Christian story as one which gives meaning to our deepest experiences. In any case, as we grow older and mature, we need to explore these grounds for ourselves in order that we can believe in God, not because we have been told to do so by our parents or teachers or friends but because faith in a loving God makes sense to us in a personal way.

"Reasons" for Believing

St. Paul blames people "of perverse and irreligious spirit" for not glorifying God although they "had knowledge of him," since "ever since the creation of the world his invisible nature, namely his eternal power and deity, has been clearly perceived in the things that have been made" (Rom. 1:18-22). But many people today have a vague feeling that, since scientists have discovered a great deal about the make-up and development of our universe and of our earth and the living things that inhabit it, the idea that Someone created and sustained all this has become outdated.

Yet, however many billions of years old and however vast the universe may be, it doesn't explain itself. If indeed it was the "big bang"—the explosion of a dense mass of matter—that began the process resulting in the world we see around us, where did that original matter come from? What started the bang? Why is anything here at all? Some people say that it is useless to ask such questions. But isn't there at least the possibility that the Beyond-being whom we call God "made" and goes on making everything that is, and for some purpose?

Along these same lines, consider the marvelous design of a snowflake or a leaf or a beetle or any living thing, and the amazing variety of them on our earth. It may have been "natural selection" or "random mutation" or some other process which produced all these things. But it isn't unreasonable to think that there is a Designer in and "behind" this process and that "the works of his hands" give us some hints about his infinite richness of life and creativity.

Different kinds of reasons for believing in God can be found by looking at our own human nature and abilities. For instance, we ask "Why?" from the time we are small children on through life. We are looking for meaning, we want to find out "what it's all about" at deeper and deeper levels. This hunger to know the meaning of life suggests that there *is* some final meaning to satisfy our desire, and that we were given this desire so that we would look for meaning.

Or again, we delight in a beautiful baseball catch, or landscape, or piece of music, or personality, and feel that in doing so we are catching a glimpse of something beyond the horizon of our everyday experience. Perhaps then, there is a "Beyond" that is, to use St. Augustine's phrase, "Beauty forever ancient and forever new."

Two ideas along this same line seem particularly helpful today, when the daily news threatens to take away our sense that life is

worthwhile. Many people find themselves unable to believe in a God who is infinite goodness because they are outraged at all the evil and suffering in the world. But where did they or anyone else first get the conviction that things should be otherwise? And why should they feel that they ought to be able to do something about intolerable situations and get angry because it seems impossible to change them? Might not the answer be that the Source of our being is also outraged by suffering and injustice—infinitely more than we are—and wants things to be different and will, with our help, somehow make them so?

Then there is the fact that, in spite of all the evil and suffering in our world, people do act in gracious and trustworthy ways. Think, for instance, how many persons must carry out their jobs conscientiously and skillfully in order for one plane to take off, fly, and land safely at a busy airport. People *are* helping one another in little ways and big, in homes, hospitals, offices, and factories. How, then, could we love and care and try to improve things unless some One at once "in" and "beyond" us were inviting and enabling us to do so? Thus both our efforts to do good things for one another and our indignation at suffering and injustice can be seen as signs of God's presence and hints as to what he is like.

Of course, none of these "reasons" or "grounds" for believing in God are proofs in the scientific sense, in the way that it can be "proved" that the earth goes around the sun. They are more like the kind of proofs we are thinking of when we talk about "proofs of love."

Thinking along the same lines, we can discover various ways in which the Christian story fits human experiences. For example, from the hints given in the Scriptures, we can certainly say that the Kingdom or Reign of God will more

than fulfill our best hopes for ourselves and those we love. It will be "life in all its fullness" (John 10:10), life in community and communion with loving and lovable people (Heb. 12:22-24), life in and with God in the glorious freedom of his children (Rom. 8:21), life vital and interesting beyond our imagining: "Eye has not seen and ear has not heard, nor has it entered into the heart of man to conceive the good things God has prepared for those who love him" (1 Cor. 2:9).

Life today certainly doesn't seem much like this Reign of God as described in the gospel. Yet it seems a little less *un*like it wherever people are trying to become their "best selves" and to help others do so. It seems a little less unlike it wherever people are trying to change situations that hinder human development. In other words, it seems a little less unlike it wherever people are trying to "walk in the ways of the Lord," the ways of justice, love, and peace. Almost everyone would agree that things would go better in our world if everyone followed these ways. Thus the kinds of attitudes and actions proposed to us in the Christian story as preparing for the Kingdom are those which we can see would help people to become more human in the positive sense—"She's a real human being!"

It may be less obvious, until you begin to think about it, that the process of becoming a mature human person involves many less or more painful "dyings" to one kind of life in order to gain a wider and freer one. Most of us do not remember much about the stages of development which we went through as small children, when we first began to realize our different relationships to the people around us. At that time, children have to give up the self-absorption and dependence proper to babies and take on new attitudes of sharing and interdependence. If they don't do this, their whole future development may well be stunted or warped. What is the major factor which helps them attain this new level? Their initial ability to trust that someone—parents and/or others—loves them just as they are. And they can only gain this ability by being so loved.

At every stage of development, people have to go through similar kinds of "dyings" to one way of living if they are to achieve a fuller and freer one. Adolescents have to give up the securities of childhood, or they remain childish and over-dependent. Young adults need to give up the "everything is ahead for me to chose from" freedom of adolescence and begin to make some serious decisions, or they may never really grow up. If they marry, they must give up the advantages as well as the disadvantages of being single, or the marriage will be a failure. And so on, up to the acceptance of old age. In all these "passages" from a familiar way of living to an unknown one, it is trust in other people's love for you which makes the "passing-over" less frightening and more complete.

Thus Jesus' passing through death to the fullness of life in the Spirit, trusting in his Father's love, and acting out of love for us, is not a pattern alien to human experience. Rather, it affirms the supreme value of trying to love other people so as to bring life out of death-like situations. It gives final meaning and purpose to all the different kinds of dying that we may have to undergo, or choose to undergo, for the sake of gaining new life for ourselves and others. It assures us that God's love is with us and for us in all these dyings, including physical death itself, and that it will bring us finally to "life in all its fullness."

To repeat: None of the ways of going from the "seen" to the "unseen" outlined in this essay prove that it is worthwhile to try to live the Christian story. But they do at least suggest that it might be. And so they enable us to give ourselves and others "reasons" for our hope, and for trying to live and celebrate the Christian story as our own.

Questions for Review:

1) Name some of the obvious reminders of the Christian story that you see in school or at home. Are there any such reminders where you work? where you recreate?

2) Why are celebrations of the Christian story so important and necessary for us when much of our time is spent with people who do not share our beliefs?

3) As we celebrate the Christian story, it is necessary to cultivate the gift of faith. How does the writer of this essay define the gift of faith? Look at the words in the Act of Faith you learned as a little child. Do you think these words say the same thing as the definition of faith in this essay?

4) What are some of the different kinds of reasons for believing in God?

5) We say in the Creed at Sunday Mass that we believe in "the life of the world to come." What are some of the hints given in the Scriptures about what this life will be like?

6) The writer of this essay, and many writers today, believe that we have to grow through many "dyings" in order to become fully mature. Give your reasons for agreeing or disagreeing with this idea of "painful passages" that help us grow into more mature human beings.

Questions for Discussion:

1) When a person says: "I have lost my faith," do you think that he or she might mean:

losing some sense of God's presence?
losing faith in some image or idea of God that no longer seems valid?
ceasing to believe in one or another formulation of a particular Christian teaching?
or something else?

If you should feel that you are "losing your faith" in any of these or other ways, what might you try to do about it?

2) Watch a documentary film on bird or animal life or life in the ocean, looking for "traces of God." What do these "traces" suggest about our responsibility for all these living creatures?

3) What would you say are some of the characteristics of "a real human being"? of a "real Christian"?

3 Journal Suggestions

Clues to God's presence are buried in our experiences of suffering as well as beauty and pleasure. The Christian story can be told starting from either point of view. The suggestions for this chapter offer you ways for getting in touch with your own hurts and healings.

4 From Sacrament to Service

The Campaign for Human Development is a unique and creative response to the troubling social problems of our day. As the introduction in the Campaign's booklet *Update '76* describes it: "The idea behind the Campaign for Human Development is powerful, direct, and profoundly Christ-like."

Begun in 1970 by the National Conference of Catholic Bishops, CHD is the Church's action/education program to attack the root causes of poverty in our society. With perhaps 40 million Americans caught in the vicious cycle of poverty, it is a courageous idea which is working.

CHD responded to the urgency of the bishops' call with a direct approach. In its history, the Campaign has funded over 1,100 self-help projects for the poor. It has provided a *way out*—not a *handout*. It has promoted human solidarity—not social division. It has offered dignity—not dependency. It has supported long-range social change—not stop-gap measures. It has gone after the structures which keep poor people poor—not the surface symptoms that mask their powerlessness.

Equally important, through the Campaign millions of individuals have reaffirmed the deep sense of justice and commitment within the American Catholic community. By the full voluntary support of the Church, all of us together have been able to offer a means of bringing people together, poor and less poor. The Campaign has been a way for us to develop, to grow—as individuals and as people. It has given us a chance to show what can be done if more of our resources are shared.

A Class Project:

Have someone in your class contact your diocesan office and ask to speak to the person in charge of the Campaign for Human Development in your area. Ask this person if he or she can visit your class at some time to describe what projects have been funded in your diocese. Or offer to visit in his or her office if this is convenient. Look at the following list of the kinds of projects which CHD funds. In what categories do the projects in your area fall?

Social Development
Health
Economic Development
Transportation
Communications
Legal Aid
Housing
Education

Then look at the list of criteria by which the CHD selects projects. Discuss these criteria with the CHD representative to see how each applies to the projects he or she describes. (If a representative from CHD is not available, your teacher can read you three separate projects funded by the CHD and you can discuss these in the light of these two lists.)

Criteria included in the form which a group seeking funding is asked to fill out.

A. Organization and Community to be Served:

1. The Campaign for Human Development addresses itself to those living in poverty. What are the predominant characteristics of the community to be served (that is, ethnic, racial, economic, etc.)?
How do you define poverty in your community?

2. How are the members of the poverty group who are being helped by the project involved in the planning, implementing, and policy-making of this project?

3. Give a brief history of the organization submitting the proposal.

B. Institutional Change:
The Campaign for Human Development defines institutional change as:

1. Modification of existing laws and/or policies.

2. Establishment of alternative structures and/or redistribution of decision-making powers;

3. Provision of services which result in the achievement of (1) and (2); or leads the recipient community to focus on (1) and (2).

4. How will this project bring about institutional change?

C. Self-Sufficiency Plans:

Will this project become economically self-sufficient if this CHD funding is made? If not, what sources of income will then sustain the project?

5 Closing Prayer

Theme:

"To Believe, To Question, To Search"

Opening Song:

"If Anyone Loves Me" by Monks of Weston Priory.

Opening Prayer:

We are a people who are searching, questioning, and trying to find a believable, real, and genuine relationship with our God. Lord Jesus, help us in our search, give us the strength and courage to listen to your word in our lives. Amen.

My Belief Statements:

Leader: I believe in a God who cares about me as a person.
All: Lord, help my unbelief.
Leader: I believe in a God who has given me life and my parents who love me.
All: Lord, help my unbelief.

Leader: I believe in a God who, like a friend, is with me through the good and rough times of my life.
All: Lord, help my unbelief.
(Additional belief statements may be added at this time.)

Reading:

A selection from *The Velveteen Rabbit*, by Margery Williams.

"What is Real?" asked the Rabbit one day, when they were lying side by side near the nursery fender, before Nana came to tidy up the room.

"Does it mean having things that buzz inside you and a stick-out handle?"

"Real isn't how you are made," said the Skin Horse, "It's a thing that happens to you. When someone loves you for a long, long time, not just to play with, but REALLY loves you, then you become Real."

"Does it hurt?" asked the Rabbit.

"Sometimes," said the Skin Horse, for he was always truthful, "When you are Real, you don't mind being hurt."

"Does it happen all at once, like being wound up," he asked, "or bit by bit?"

"It doesn't happen all at once," said the Skin Horse. "You become. It takes a long time. That's why it doesn't often happen to people who break easily, or have sharp edges, or who have to be carefully kept. Generally, by the time you're Real, most of your hair has been loved off, and your eyes drop out, and you get loose in the joints and very shabby. But these things don't matter at all, because once you are Real you can't be ugly, except to people who don't understand."

We are now at our beginning . . .
You are making it happen . . .
Help us become . . .
Real!

Reflection:

What is real for me?
What do I believe about my God?

Closing Song:

"A Creed" by Joe Wise.

Learning to Live
the Story

Chapter 4

1 Orientation

At some time now or in the future, all of us begin to consider those ways in which we will make a "living" or make a "livelihood." The distinction between the two words is not an arbitrary one. Usually, making a living involves getting a job by which we can become financially self-sufficient. The need to make a livelihood, on the other hand, can involve a broader range of choices. It can include decisions not only about the work we want to do but about the kind of lifestyle we want to adopt. What values will we follow? How will we develop friendships? How will we make what we do count? What do we hope to contribute to the betterment of the whole community?

Whenever we start to ask questions like these, we are responding to Jesus' request that we become "Kingdom-builders." Throughout his life, in his actions and in his teaching, Jesus preached about the Kingdom. But he was not talking about an out-of-this-world utopia. His call to work for the coming of the Kingdom was a call to bring about a new state of affairs in *this* world by transforming people's vision of the way they ought to live. Jesus wished to bring about a new order of things in which gospel values of peace and justice, mercy and compassion, goodness and truth would govern our attitudes and life-styles.

How do we participate in this on-going process of building the Kingdom? Whenever we act out of a spirit of love and concern for others, whether this involves the seemingly small tasks of helping with housework or carrying out our school responsibilities, we are hastening the advent of God's Kingdom. But since Christianity is a call to commit our lives to the values of the gospel in a long-range way, we need to consider the direction of our future choices.

Decisions about occupational and vocational goals are not easily made. They tend to change as our own interests and experiences develop and widen. But since so many of our future hopes and plans are being determined by the various choices we make in high school, it is important to reflect on the kinds of talents, abilities, and gifts we have now. What occupations interest us personally? Take some time to think about the following questions. You might write your responses to them in your journal.

Forgetting about money, what would you like to do more than anything else?

Where and with what kinds of people can you work most effectively?

What is the most challenging job you can think of?

What talents and abilities do you have now?

What talents and abilities would you like to have and how would you go about achieving these?

What would you like to do in the future?

2 Reading and Discussion

Learning to Live the Story

A traveler in medieval times saw three men near the road cutting stone. He asked them what they were doing. The first said grumpily, "Cutting stone." The second said matter-of-factly, "Earning a living." The third said enthusiastically, "Building a cathedral!"

Obviously, there isn't much point in celebrating the Christian story unless we are trying to live it. But if we try consciously to take part in it, we can lead our lives like the third man, with gusto. For we can see our efforts to "walk in God's ways" as providing building materials for the Kingdom of God.

This is true because we have been given the Spirit of Jesus, the Spirit who enables us to call God "Father" and to act as his children, following his ways. As we allow the Spirit to form and vivify us, we are "one Spirit" with our Risen Lord. What we do is at once his work and ours; it is the continuation of his work in today's world. Even though we may not *feel* very enthusiastic much of the time, the hope and courage given us by our conviction that life is really worthwhile can be a kind of undercurrent, carrying us along, keeping us going.

But to take part in the story purposefully, we need to try to shape our attitudes and actions so that they can be building materials for the Kingdom. We need to follow God's ways as described in the Scriptures. They are paths to fullness of life in communion with God and other persons and all creation. These ways are uniquely exemplified in Jesus, who is himself "the Way." The gospels show him healing people of diseases of spirit and body, giving respect and welcome to outcasts. They show him feeding hungry crowds and supplying good wine at a wedding when the host's supply had given out. They show him eating and drinking with both "respectable" and "disreputable" people. They show him observant and appreciative of different kinds of human behavior, and of his Father's work in "clothing" field grasses with flowers and feeding the birds of the air. They show him praying. And they show him weary, indignant, fearful, suffering, and dying.

During his public ministry Jesus was thus preparing for the Kingdom and was teaching us how to do so by what he was and what he did, as well as by what he said. But he must also have been learning and following God's ways, his Father's ways, during all the years of his growing up and working as a carpenter in Nazareth. Moreover, he must have done so in a very "ordinary," unobtrusive fashion. Otherwise when he began to teach and heal, his fellow villagers wouldn't have asked, "Where did this man get this wisdom and these mighty works?" (Matthew 13:54).

Most of our Kingdom-building actions are of this "ordinary" kind: trying to discover who we are and trying to develop our abilities . . . going out of ourselves in small acts of kindness, forgiveness, love . . . trying to respect and deal considerately with the persons with whom we live and work and play . . . putting up with failures and frustrations and pains . . . learning to delight in what is truly delightful.

But however ordinary such efforts seem, they involve making more or less difficult choices against giving in to our own selfishness, laziness, desire to do what "everyone" is doing—all the kinds of giving-in that keep us imprisoned in ourselves and in comfortably familiar situations, rather than affording us the freedom of God's children.

Guidelines for Decision-making

Moreover, such efforts also involve making decisions as to what is a Kingdom-building course of action in a particular situation—by no means an easy task in our complex world. For example, one's work should obviously be one's chief means of providing building-materials for the Kingdom, through loving and skillful service to some real human need. It should also be work which engages and develops one's capabilities the better to serve these needs as well as one's own. But many kinds of work today serve artificial wants of relatively affluent people in affluent countries, and do so at the expense of poor people in poor countries and of the poor in our country. Again, many occupations today, from assembly-line work to banking, offer no opportunities for true human growth. As Studs Terkel put it in his book *Working*, "Most of us have jobs that are too small for our spirit." And many people have no jobs at all.

Young people, then, have to make difficult decisions about what kinds of occupations to fit themselves for and what kinds of life-styles will contribute to their own happiness and at the same time in some way benefit our problem-ridden society. Older people who are beginning to realize their responsibility to help prepare for the Kingdom have to decide how to make a living, while trying to change those aspects of "the system" which are destructive of human well-being.

And then, of course, there are all the decisions we have to make about our personal relationships: what is the loving thing to do for a particular person in these particular circumstances, without acting unlovingly toward someone else? And there are many kinds of decisions we have to make about matters of daily concern as well as critical questions of life and death.

Happily, though the responsibility for making decisions is finally ours, we do not have to make them all on our own. We belong to the community of the church and to the community of people of good will. In both these communities, the Spirit of Jesus is at work enabling their members to help one another choose and carry out what will prepare for the Kingdom. How we can know that we are following God's ways, Jesus' ways, with the help of these communities and the Spirit is well summarized in the following excerpt from the book *How Do I Know I'm Doing Right?* by Gerard Sloyan.

I know I'm doing right if I try to be pure in intention in all that I do—what Jesus called being "single-minded" (see Matthew 5:8).

I know I'm doing right if I consult the teaching of Jesus Christ, Lord of the church, in his own words in the New Testament, and Moses and the prophets whom Jesus relied on, and Paul and those other apostles who taught in Jesus' name.

I know I'm doing right when I consciously make my love for God through my concern for individuals (*this* man, *this* woman) the measuring-stick for every choice.

I know I'm doing right when I consult the church to help me resolve my conscience: its bishop-teachers, its theologians and religious thinkers, its holy and learned members of my own acquaintance. In all that I do, I mean to seek the counsel of the brotherhood of believers—not theirs alone but that of any person of goodwill.

I know I'm doing right when I remain faithful to my conscience, which I have done everything in my power to inform.

I know I'm doing right if I follow with care current debate on the great contemporary moral issues heavy with social implications, on which the church has not been able to make a final judgment. I am the church, and my brothers and sisters need my help in this just as I need theirs.

I know I'm doing right if I pray for the grace of God in all that I do.

I know I'm doing right if I conceive sorrow for my sinfulness and not only for my sins. I must confess my serious sins humbly and sincerely, neither withholding them nor excusing them.

I know I'm doing right if I ask the Holy Spirit to make me a creature of love, a loving person in the human family and in the church; cleaving to what is right, rejecting what is wrong without fear or favor or human respect. What the Spirit *can* do in me to conform me to Christ as a child of the Father, *that* I ask that He *do* do.

The Lord Is with Us

Thus to the Christian, the Kingdom-building way of looking at our lives and actions not only gives them final value and purpose, it also gives us the assurance that we are not alone. The stone-cutter who knew that he was building a cathedral could feel himself one of a great com-

munity of persons having different skills, all working to make a beautiful "house of God." So we can realize that we are members of the community of all persons of good will who are working for the Kingdom, in the Spirit, however they may express what they are doing. And we can realize that we belong to the community of all those who—in the present, past, and future—call Jesus "Lord" and believe that he is the master-builder of what the Book of Revelation calls "the home of God with men" (21:3).

But our Risen Lord isn't like an architect who makes plans and leaves it to others to carry them out. Nor is he like a supervisor who comes around occasionally to check on the progress of a building. We are each, and all together, "one in the Spirit" with him. And so he is working in us and with us to carry out his Father's loving purpose for humankind and all creation.

However, there are different ways of being with another person. Two close friends may be working at the same task—painting a room, getting a meal ready. They can be aware of and happy in each other's companionship, while at the same time concentrating on their work. Then they may also stop what they are doing and take time simply to be with each other, to talk together, to share experiences, to enjoy each other.

So, as we go about our various occupations, we can be with our Risen Lord in the first way. But we also need to take some time to be with him in the second way. He understands our experiences "from inside," as one of us. Now, in his risen life he is with us in the very nearness of God. So we can simply try to realize his nearness and his love for us, or share our experiences with him in whatever way seems most comfortable. And with him, we can dare to let ourselves realize and respond to the Presence of the Father.

Jesus is with and for each of us, whether we are alone or with other people. But he has promised to be present with us in a special way "wherever two or three are gathered together in my name." Since in the Kingdom all will be one with him as he is one with the Father, he wants his followers to be community-builders and to find him in community.

Christians gather together in the name of Jesus for many purposes—to give one another mutual support, to become more familiar with the Christian story as their own story, to plan and carry out Kingdom-building actions. But there is one kind of gathering which focuses all these elements of Christian living in a very special way—coming together to celebrate the Christian story, with Jesus, in the Spirit, to the glory of the Father: what we today call "sacramental celebrations."

As was pointed out in the first of these essays, a celebration involves a symbolic action conveying meaning beyond the physical facts. The word "sacrament" also has come, by a complex process, to stand for this same kind of "sign."

St. Paul calls the story "the mystery of Christ." But the Greek word *musterion*, as it is used in the Scriptures, doesn't mean what we do when we say, "That's a mystery to me!" On the contrary, it means a revelation, a showing-forth, of what had been previously hidden in God's wisdom. The Christian story, then, is the "mystery"—the manifestation of God's loving purposes in and through Jesus Christ. So the term *mysteria* came to be used for celebrations which re-present the story in symbolic sign-language. Official church documents still use the phrase, "celebrating the sacred mysteries."

When Latin-speaking Christians needed a term for these same celebrations, they chose *sacramentum*—a word which originally stood for the ceremonies, including a solemn oath of allegiance, which men went through before joining the Roman Army. Later the term came to be applied to a wide variety of "sacred signs," until the Council of Trent limited its use to the seven sacraments of present Catholic practice.

But St. Paul's original phrase, "the mystery of Christ," applies both to the whole story and to Jesus himself as the unique and perfect human "sign" or manifestation of God. So the term "sacrament" can be used of him also; a modern theologian, for instance, calls one of his works, *Christ, the Sacrament of Our Encounter with God*. Along the same lines, the church is called a sacrament, since it is meant to be, through its life and actions, a sign of God's love revealed and given in Christ. And all of us are to try to be such signs to one another.

It might be said, then, that "the" sacraments are meant to help *us* become sacraments. But they do not work like magic. We have to dispose ourselves by trying to do what has been discussed in these essays: becoming more and more familiar with the story as our story and trying to live it with Jesus as members of the Christian and human communities. And we also need to explore the meanings of the symbolic signs that re-present the story and its implications for our lives. The sacraments "effect what they signify." But we can hardly be affected by them if their sign-language doesn't convey anything to us. These meanings are, then, what we will be exploring in the four following essays.

Questions for Review:

1) Why was the third stone-cutter able to work enthusiastically?

2) Why should we be able to live hopefully?

3) What were some of the things Jesus did to prepare for the Kingdom and to teach us how to do so?

4) What are some of the ordinary things we can do so that our actions and attitudes will help build the Kingdom of God here on earth?

5) What things sometimes make it difficult to have good attitudes and to take good actions?

6) What are some things we need to consider when making decisions about our work and about personal relationships?

7) How does the Christian Kingdom-building way of looking at our lives and our actions give them final value and purpose and also give us the assurance that we are not alone?

Questions for Discussion:

1) What institutions, forces, or trends in our society do you think make it especially difficult to live the Christian story? Which ones make it difficult for *you*?

2) How might you begin to use the criteria given on page 36 in solving daily problems about "doing right"?

3) Jesus told a parable (Luke 18:1-5) to teach us that we should "pray without ceasing." How is this possible?

4) A modern theologian has written about "the sacrament of the brother"—"brother" meaning every other human person. What do you think he means?

3 Journal Suggestions

People all around you are living the Christian story in many ways and so are you. Much of our behavior during any day is a kind of "Kingdom-building." Follow the Journal Suggestions for this chapter to see more clearly how you already live the story.

4 From Sacrament to Service

People reveal a variety of reasons for selecting a particular job or occupation. They may be motivated by the need for money, prestige, self-fulfillment. But one of the most common questions people have about their work is: "Does it make any difference?" Unfortunately, too many Americans suffer from a feeling that what they do really makes little difference. They feel that their jobs are often routine, uninteresting, unimportant. In a book which describes the feelings that many Americans have about their different jobs, Studs Terkel, a Chicago radio reporter, interviewed hundreds of Americans about the feelings they had toward their work and published their stories in a book called *Working*. In the very first account, a steelworker talks about his need to feel that what he does makes a difference. He says:

"Somebody built the pyramids. Somebody's going to build something. Pyramids. Empire State Building—these things just don't happen. There's hard work behind it. I would like to see a building, say, the Empire State, I would like to see on one side of it a foot-wide strip from top to bottom with the name of every bricklayer, the name of every electrician, with all the names. So when a guy walked by he could take his son and say, 'See, that's me over there on the forty-fifth floor. I put the steel beam in.' Picasso can point to a painting. What can I point to? A writer can point to a book. Everybody should have something to point to."

What do you think about the statement of the steelworker that *everybody should have something to point to*? Later in the interview, the steelworker fantasizes about what he would do if he could really do anything he wanted. He says:

"I'd like to run a combination bookstore and tavern. I would like to have a place where college kids came and a steelworker could sit down and talk.

"Where a workingman could not be ashamed of Walt Whitman and where a college professor could not be ashamed that he painted his house over a weekend.

"If a carpenter built a cabin for poets, I think the least the poets owe the carpenter is just three or four one-liners on the wall. A little plaque: Though we labor with our minds, this place we can relax in was built by someone who can work with his hands. And his work is as noble as ours. I think the poet owes something to the guy who builds the cabin for him."

The steelworker knows that most of the time carpenters and poets do not meet each other in their work worlds. There seems to be a certain bias built into the nature of American work. For example, doctors and sanitation workers both contribute to the health of communities. Indeed if sanitation workers failed to collect the city's garbage, all kinds of diseases would be rampant. But few would deny that doctors are esteemed and sanitation workers are not.

Those who live by gospel values and who are working to bring about God's Kingdom do not have to conform to the values of their culture. With the help of your classmates, write down on the blackboard twenty occupations. Discuss how these occupations further the coming of God's Kingdom.

5 Closing Prayer

Theme:

Happy are they who live the Good News!

Opening Song:

"Whatsoever You Do"

Reflection:

Jesus' message and the Christian mission are summarized in what is called "The Sermon on the Mount." Take a few moments to think about these questions:

What is happiness?

What would really make you happy?

Reading:

Now let us listen to Jesus' words on what Christian happiness can mean. A reading from the Good News according to Matthew.

Seeing the crowds, he went up on the mountain, and when he sat down his disciples came to him. And he opened his mouth and taught them, saying:

"Blessed are the poor in spirit, for theirs is the kingdom of heaven."
"Blessed are those who mourn, for they shall be comforted.
"Blessed are the meek, for they shall inherit the earth.
"Blessed are those who hunger and thirst for righteousness, for they shall be satisfied.
"Blessed are the merciful, for they shall obtain mercy.
"Blessed are the pure in heart, for they shall see God.
"Blessed are the peacemakers, for they shall be called sons of God.
"Blessed are those who are persecuted for righteousness' sake, for theirs is the kingdom of heaven" (5:1-10).

Response:

Right Side: Happy are those who are ready to share what they have with others.
Left Side: Lord, help me deserve this happiness.
Right Side: Happy are those who graciously accept what others have to give.
Left Side: Lord, help me deserve this happiness.

Right Side: Happy are those who make others feel like insiders.
Left Side: Lord, help me deserve this happiness.
(Additional prayers may be added at this time.)

Meditation:

Either use the film *Theirs Is the Kingdom* or make your own slide/music presentation on people helping others.

Reflection:

Think of some concrete action you can perform this week which might deserve the happiness Jesus promises.

Leader:

(Clasp hands in a circle, as a sign of our community.) Let us pray the prayer that Jesus taught us to pray: "Our Father . . .

Closing Song:

"Whatsoever You Do"

The Eucharist:
Celebrating the Whole Story

Chapter 5

1 Orientation

In 1911, a member of the Yahi tribe of California Indians was rediscovered to the white man's world. The Yahi had not been heard from in forty years, and it was assumed that they had been wiped out in massacres by gold-seekers.

Theodora Kroeber and her family became friends with this Indian. In *Ishi, Last of His Tribe*, she recounts the life of his small band and how they dwindled until Ishi became the last survivor of his people. Drawn from Ishi's own words, the book describes how the band hunted, fished, and gathered food almost invisibly in their little valley. Because they feared being discovered by white men, they lived in hiding and they blended their activities into the forest sounds. For instance, to cut a tree branch for making a hunting bow took hours, for it was severed "with only such sounds as the rubbing and snapping of branches make in the wind." Yet the band maintained their traditions, their "Way of Life," and their relationships were of a caring and generous kind.

Most important to Ishi was his position as hunter for the band. Being hunter was a role of both social and religious significance for the Yahi. Often he would speak of himself in this way: "A hunter retrieves his arrow. It takes much work to make an arrow, and the arrowhead is treasure."

As drastically different as the Yahi way of life is from our own, it shares with ours certain things important to community-building. According to the theologian David O'Neill, "the richest experiencing of community comes when there is a conscious sharing, with dedication and commitment, at three levels . . ." These levels are: (1) *meaning*, which for Ishi was his role as the hunter, (2) *task* or effort on behalf of the community, and (3) *celebration*, which for the Yahi were the Harvest Feasts at the end of the hunting and gathering seasons.

Community works on these same three levels in our own lives.

Meaning: All of the groups we belong to—family, friends, class, club, church, school, teams—have a set of purposes which means something to the people involved. A family, for instance, can have meaning as a group dedicated to respecting each member, to helping each other grow physically and spiritually, to caring for each other's needs, to reaching out to help others, and so on.

Task: The purposes of a community make the efforts that go into building and sustaining it worthwhile. Think of all the work that goes into organizing a prom or a homecoming dance. Have you ever been in a bike marathon or helped to organize one? Are such efforts worthwhile?

Celebration: Group effort toward some shared purpose is always cause for celebration. Whether it is putting up an art exhibit, building a float for the school parade, working for a state cross country title or a chess championship, some kind of celebration is bound to follow accomplishment. These celebrations might be refreshments at someone's house or supper and speeches at a fancy restaurant.

The essay which follows deals with the Eucharist as the celebration of the Christian community. Before you read the essay, try to grasp how celebration is experienced in relation to the other two levels of community.

2 Reading and Discussion

Celebrating the Whole Story

Sharing food and drink seems to be a universal human sign of sharing life and what is necessary for life. In many cultures, for example, to share a meal is a pledge of friendship and mutual aid. To invite a stranger to a meal is a commitment to treat him or her as "one of us." We ourselves feel that eating and drinking together is the appropriate setting for sharing ideas and plans and hopes, or simply for enjoying one another's company. We consider "refreshments" a most important part of almost any kind of gathering.

Why should human beings feel this way about such an ordinary human action? Obviously because—as all the starving and undernourished people in the world know only too well—food and drink literally do mean life and health.

Again, if you have ever tried to cultivate even a small vegetable garden, you know something about how producing food is dependent on the soil and the weather. And you have some notion of how much human toil is involved: eating presupposes an enormous amount of working.

Thus *sharing* food and drink means sharing life and health, sharing the resources of our earth, and sharing in life-producing labor. And sharing the best food and drink available, as we do at a festive meal, symbolizes the desire to make life not only possible for one another, but also attractive and enjoyable. In brief, sharing food and drink means "community" in its fullest sense.

Sharing the Eucharistic bread and wine is, then, the most appropriate action possible for showing us what God wants to be to us and to do for us, *and* what he wants us to be to one another and do for one another. Jesus gives us his own self ("my Body") for our food and his very life ("my Blood") so that we may truly live as one community, sharing his life with the Father in the Spirit. And in doing so he shows us how we are to share ourselves, our talents, our resources with others—with all the "dyings" involved in doing so—in order to nourish and increase their lives and our own. And so the Eucharistic meal signifies God's desire to give us, through Jesus, "life in all its fullness" (John 10:10), a life of delight and joyful activity—the life which will be that of the Kingdom and which we should be trying to foster here and now.

Bread and Wine

Such meanings of sharing food and drink are intensified and focused in sharing bread and wine. In the Mediterranean culture in which Jesus lived, bread was the basic staple food (and it was really nourishing food, unlike so much of the bread we eat in the United States). So it was particularly suited to stand for everything people need for life and health. "Give us this day our daily bread" means "Give us all that we need." In the same sense, we ourselves use such phrases as "How many bread-winners are there in this family?" "She doesn't know which side her bread is buttered on," and "Taking bread out of a person's mouth."

In that same culture, wine was the usual festive drink. And so it was particularly suited to stand for all kinds of life-enhancing, gladdening actions.

Further, any kinds of foods or drinks made from grains and fruits remind us that, as Jesus said, "Unless a grain of wheat falls into the ground and dies, it remains alone; but if it does it bears much fruit" (John 12:24).

Finally, the early Christians discovered still another meaning. Many grains are ground up together and baked to make one loaf, and many grapes crushed and fermented to make a cup of wine. So individual Christians are to become one in Christ through the power of his Spirit—one community which would commit itself to serve others as he did.

Thus the human meanings of sharing food and drink, and particularly bread and wine, open out the meanings of the Eucharist. These meanings then gain new and deeper dimensions from the use of bread and wine in the Passover meal which was the framework for the Last Supper.

The Passover Meal

The key event in the Jewish story, as was mentioned earlier, is the Exodus: God's saving his people from slavery in Egypt, making a covenant with them on Mount Sinai, and bringing them through the desert to the Promised Land. The Passover meal is the yearly celebration of these wonderful deeds, a celebration which the

LORD commanded when they first went out of Egypt. Before the main course of roasted lamb, a special blessing is said over unleavened bread. And at the end of the meal, another blessing is said over a cup of wine—both shared by all those present.

These blessings are prayers praising and thanking the LORD for all his wonderful deeds and particularly for the events of the Exodus. And each Jewish group which celebrates a Passover meal thinks of the Exodus experience, not only as what happened to the Hebrew people long ago but as somehow also their own experience. These blessings then end with a plea to the LORD to fulfill his promises made to the prophets by sending his Messiah to inaugurate the Kingdom of God.

Thus this meal celebrates the whole Jewish story, past, present, and future. And by taking part in it, Jewish families and groups personally and communally renew their commitment to the covenant made on Mount Sinai between the LORD and the Hebrew people.

"Covenant" sounds to us like a legal word, like "contract." But it actually means something more and different in Jewish and Christian usage. It is not simply a matter of "I'll do this if you'll do that." A covenant establishes a new *relationship* between the parties, based on mutual promises. The Hebrew people, then, heard Moses read to them the Law that the LORD wished them to live by and his promise to be with them and for them as their God if they would do so. When they had shouted their agreement, Moses had animals slain and their blood sprinkled on an altar, representing the LORD, and on the people. Since in biblical thinking blood means life, this gesture signified the living union between the LORD and his people, created by his covenant with them.

Thus the various ritual sacrifices which we read about in the Scriptures had, like the Passover meal, the purpose of renewing this covenant relationship. "Sacrifice" literally means "making holy"—entering into God's sphere of life, so to speak. These sacrifices, then, expressed the offerers' desire to be "at one" with God, offering animal victims or foods of different kinds to stand for their own lives. In some cases, the offerers shared with the priests in eating the meat that now belonged to God—a sign of the offerers' renewed at-one-ness with him.

In the Passover meal, sharing food and drink become signs both of the LORD's and of the participants' continued commitment to the covenant. The meal is a sign of the life-giving and life-sharing acts of the LORD for his people and his continued presence with them and for them. And they are also signs of the life-giving and life-sharing acts and behavior laid out in the Law, the "ways of the LORD" which his people promise to follow to be at one with him.

It was this meal, with all its wealth of meaning, in which Jesus, as the leader of a new Exodus, celebrated his own "passage" to the Father, bringing about a new covenant between God and all humankind.

The Last Supper

"And when the hour came, he sat at table and the apostles with him. And he said to them, 'I have earnestly desired to eat this passover with you before I suffer; for I tell you I shall not eat it until it is fulfilled in the kingdom of God.' . . . And he took bread, and when he had given thanks he broke it and gave it to them, saying 'This is my body which is given for you. Do this in remembrance of me.' And likewise the cup after supper, saying, 'This cup which is poured out for you is the covenant in my blood'" (Luke 22:14-20).

When Jesus "gave thanks" he was offering the "blessings" to be said over bread and wine at the Passover meal. He praised and thanked his Father for all the wonderful works done for his people, the Jews. But he also gave thanks and praise for the still more wonderful work to be accomplished for all humankind by his going through death, trusting in the Father to give him a new life, the life of the Kingdom. This "Exodus" through death to the Father establishes a new covenant, a new life-sharing relationship, between God and humans. And the sign of this Exodus and its effects was his giving himself ("my body") to his disciples in the form of bread, and his very life ("my blood") in the form of wine. In this sign, he wholly gave himself to God and to human persons "so that all may be one" (John 17:22-23).

Thus he gathered up all the life-giving and life-sharing meanings of bread and wine to celebrate the whole Christian story, past, present, and future, to show us how to take part in it, and to enable us to do so. And he continues to do this in every Eucharist (the word means giving "thanks and praise").

Taking Part in Jesus' Eucharist

Through the centuries since Jesus' death and glorification, Christian communities have continued to "Do this" as he commanded, convinced of the special presence of their Risen Lord in this celebration. They have always retained the central action: giving thanks and praise to the Father, with and through Jesus, in a prayer over bread and wine which includes an account and re-presentation of what Jesus said and did at the Last Supper, followed by eating the bread and drinking the wine.

But there have been, and are today, many different "rites," or prescribed ways, of carrying out this action, with many and varied additions. For just as there are many ways of telling the Christian story, so there are many ways of celebrating it. No one way could be "the way" because people of different cultures perceive and do things differently. The "best" way is the one which most directly and richly conveys the many interwoven meanings of the Eucharist to those who celebrate it.

Our own Roman rite may itself be celebrated in many different styles, and with some variations. One of these, which is most desirable for small groups, is to use bread which looks and tastes like bread and can be broken to share among the participants—for example, a round, flat, unleavened Armenian loaf. Taking part in such a Eucharist enables people actually to share food and drink, rather than simply to receive the token wafer necessary at large parish Masses.

To choose and carry out the kind of liturgy best suited to a given group is the responsibility of liturgy planning committees, the chief celebrant, the lector, and so on. And how the Roman Rite might be more radically adapted to the needs of different groups and cultures is, ultimately, the responsibility of the Pope and the bishops, aided by experts in various fields. But what we can all do, as these essays have tried to point out, is to become more and more familiar with the Christian story, to try to live it, and then to come to each Mass to celebrate it.

Of course, we can't expect to feel a great surge of love for God and our neighbors whenever we go to Mass. But we can expect to be "made more Christian" if we really try to take our part in it. This involves more than making the responses and joining in the singing. We need to realize, in faith, that we are joining in *Jesus'* giving thanks and praise to the Father. He is the chief celebrant, inviting us to share in his own joy in God's great work for our salvation, to be finally completed in the life of the Kingdom, the life which he is already living. This is why so many prayers in the Mass and, above all, the Eucharistic Prayer, are offered "through Christ our Lord."

We are also celebrating this great work with a particular church community *and* with all other human persons concerned in this work. This is why so many people, living and dead, are mentioned in the Eucharistic Prayers. We are one in the Spirit with a vast community, many of whom have already "entered into the joy of their Lord" (Matthew 25:23).

And since we are trying—however imperfectly—to follow Jesus' way, whatever we do and endure in his Spirit is being celebrated in the celebration of his great work. To bring out this aspect of our participation is one of the reasons for the offering of the bread and wine to the Father before the Eucharistic Prayer: the bread and wine stand for us and our contribution to the Christian story.

This is also the sense of the language of sacrifice used in the Mass, in some hymns, and in much traditional instruction—language which needs to be properly understood if it is not to repel us. The word "host," for example, means "victim"—and who wants to be a "victim" in the sense we usually take it? Jesus' death was a sacrifice in which he was the "victim" in the sense explained earlier, and this sacrifice actually achieved the "at-one-ness" with God which was the intention of the Temple animal sacrifices (see Hebrews 8:10-25). The Eucharistic celebration re-presents this unique sacrifice and, included in it, our own efforts to be "at one" with God and with other people.

To prepare for the Eucharistic celebration, we take part in the Liturgy of the Word, which brings out one or another aspect of the Eucharist's wealth of meaning for us. When we hear and respond to the Readings, we need to ask ourselves: What is Jesus, present in this Word, telling me about my life, my part in the story, through these passages from Scripture?

For example, every Eucharist obviously speaks to us about the starving and undernourished millions in our world and about all the problems involved in food production and distribution. Our taking part in the Eucharist, then, commits us to doing whatever we can to feed the hungry and help the hungry feed themselves. It also commits us to take what opportunities are open to us to study the complex issues involved in a just distribution of food and of the means to produce food, and to find means that will not destroy our earth.

And also, as I hope this essay has brought out, taking part in the Eucharist should give us the assurance that such efforts really are worthwhile, though they seem so insignificant, for it celebrates the *whole* Christian story, anticipating the Kingdom in which "all will be well."

Questions for Review:

1) In the celebration of the Eucharist, Jesus makes himself our shared food and drink. What does this show us about what he wants to be to us and to do for us?

2) What was the nature of the covenant made on Mount Sinai between the LORD and the Hebrew people?

3) What does the Jewish Passover meal celebrate?

4) What was celebrated at the Last Supper and continues to be celebrated in the Eucharist?

5) What are the essential elements of the Eucharistic celebration?

Questions for Discussion:

1) Before beginning the Eucharistic Prayer, the presiding celebrant says to the other participants, "Pray that my sacrifice and yours may be acceptable to God the Father almighty." How is a Eucharistic celebration in which you take part *your* sacrifice?

2) What are some of the ways in which you can help to "make" a Eucharistic celebration you take part in?

3) What are some of the ways in which taking part in the Eucharist should "make Christians"?

3 Journal Suggestions

Meals are a way of "sharing life," a way of celebrating togetherness, someone's renewed presence, or an accomplishment. The suggestions for this chapter will help you tune in to meals as celebrations.

4 From Sacrament to Service

The study of the Eucharist helps us understand that as Eucharistic people, who have been greatly blessed, greatly gifted, we are called to share. Sometimes we share things that we have in abundance, and if we are selfish, that sharing is hard. There are other times when we are called to share when there doesn't seem to be enough for our own needs—when we are called to limit our own use of something so others may have even a little—when we are called to "spare and share."

"Never before have so many suffered so much from hunger. . . . Over one-half of the human race exists in conditions of chronic poverty that keep them underfed and uncertain about their next meal. Growing num-

bers are convinced that their plight need not be so desperate—that if the earth's resources were justly utilized, there would be food for all. They hunger for bread and justice" (*Christian Responsibility in a Hungry World*).

These "growing numbers" are quite right. "There is no such thing as absolute scarcity. Every country in the world has the capacity to feed itself" (*Bread First*). But before the forces which have brought about and continue the present situation can be persuaded to change their ways, more and more of us have to understand how these forces work and find ways of influencing them. The following activities, then, may help you enter a little into the frustrations and desperation of those who are really poor.

The class will be divided into three groups with approximately the same number of students in each group. Each group is to prepare a report to present to the class. Included in the report should be anything which will make the facts you have gathered seem more real—pictures, interviews with people, articles, and so on.

Group One:
Look through newspapers and magazines for accounts of people in our own country or in any other country who are suffering because there is not a fair distribution of food, grain, water, medicine, or housing.

Group Two:
Select one of the following people to interview: a restaurant manager; a

"fast foods" manager (hamburger or pizza place, for example); a cook in a school hot lunch program; the manager of a grocery store or a supermarket. Ask these people about the food that is wasted at their place of work. What steps have been taken to cut down on wasted food? Who are the biggest "offenders" in food waste? What happens to food that has been prepared or stocked on shelves and is not sold? Could it be distributed to poor families before it is unusable? Do they have any way of estimating about how much food is wasted in a week? How do they feel about wasted food?

Group Three:
Find out how much food is wasted at your homes in a week. Instead of cleaning the uneaten food off the plates into a garbage disposal or into a garbage pail, have a one or two quart container ready and put all the wasted food from the plates into it following a meal. How many quart containers of wasted food did you count in a week? Could some of this waste be avoided?

5 Para-Liturgy

Theme:

"I Am the Bread of Life"

Opening Song:

"I Am the Bread of Life" by Sr. M. Suzanne Toolan, S.M.

Leader:

Jesus of Nazareth invites you to a meal to break bread with your brothers, sisters, family, friends, and neighbors. Will you attend?

Pray Together:

Lord Jesus, we come together today to share our gifts. Help us to realize the real meaning of bread and how important food and your food is for us as Christian people growing in our love for you. Amen.

Reading:

A reading from the Good News according to John. At that time, Jesus said to the people:

"I am the bread of life; he who comes to me shall not hunger, and he who believes in me shall never thirst. . . . I am the living bread which came down from heaven; if anyone eats of this bread he will live forever; and the bread which I shall give for the life of the world is my flesh . . . he who eats my flesh and drinks my blood abides in me and I in him. As the living Father has sent me, and I live because of the Father, so he who eats me will live because of me. . . . He who eats this bread will live forever" (6:48 ff).

Shared Prayer:

You are invited to share your insights or to share prayer.

Pray Together:

We want to share bread with each person here today . . . and as we break bread . . . we give thanks to our God for sharing with us his Son, Jesus Christ. Amen.

Ritual:

Each person is invited to break off a piece of bread and eat it.

Prayers of the Community:

Right Side: Lord, I give thanks for the times that others have helped me to experience your love.

Left Side: Help me become bread for others.

Right Side: Lord, I give thanks for the food that I have to eat each day.

Left Side: Help me become bread for others.

Right Side: Lord, I give thanks for the opportunity to receive a good education.

Left Side: Help me become bread for others.
(Additional prayers may be added at this time.)

Pray Together:

O God, who sent your Son into the world to show your love, may we as your people invite our friends, relatives, and neighbors and share with them the Love that we have received from you, our God. This we ask in your name. Amen.

Closing Song:

"Jesus Is Life" by Rev. Carey Landry.

Baptism and Confirmation:
Celebrations of Becoming Insiders

Chapter 6

1 Orientation

As youngsters we were totally un-aware that our families had any other purpose than to fulfill our own wants and wishes. Nor did we actively con-tribute to the upkeep of our families. As we grew older, though, we were expected more and more to lend a hand to household chores and to help plan family activities. We became more conscious of the other members of the family and of the values and needs of the family as a whole, as a community.

Sometime during high school, how-ever, things change again. We begin to see ourselves as persons in our own right, independent of the family. And while we often regard other family members highly, at the same time we seek the freedom to discover and de-velop our selves—our talents, our perspectives, our values. This process is confusing and sometimes painfully bewildering. We often feel trapped and we feel badly about failing our duties as family members.

What we don't fully realize is the complexity of our roles as family members. These roles are the "hats" we wear—mother, brother, sister, daughter. And we all wear more than one such hat. Your father, for instance, also lives the role of a husband. Sort-ing out your roles and those of other family members can help you get a handle on the feeling of entanglement you might be experiencing. You might discover also that living as a family member isn't easy for anyone in your family.

A Family Map

On a separate sheet of paper, draw your family map. First, at the top of the map, draw a face for each adult member of your family. If you have a grandparent living with you, add his or her face to the row of adults. If one parent is dead or not living with you, represent him or her with a filled-in circle. Anyone who has ever been a part of the family leaves an effect on the others. Now draw faces for your-self, your brothers and sisters.

Connect all of your family members with arrows to show the various roles. For instance, you would draw one arrow from your mother to you to in-dicate her role as a mother to you. You would draw another arrow from you to your mother because you act to her in the role of a son or a daughter. When you have drawn in all of the possible roles, you will begin to see the compli-cated network of roles that exists even in an average-sized family. In a family of five people, for instance, twenty arrows would be needed to indicate all the roles.

The following essay deals with the sacraments which celebrate our be-coming insiders to the Christian story and to the Christian community. Take a moment before reading the essay to ask yourself in what ways being an insider to your family affects you as a Christian. Can the Christian story or the larger Christian commu-nity help you make sense of your family roles?

2 Reading and Discussion

Celebrations of Becoming Insiders

When you think about the process of becoming an insider in any community which includes people of all ages, you realize that there are two main ways of doing so. For example, if you are born in a small town, with parents who take part in its affairs, you are accepted as an insider from the start. You become a more actively in-volved member of the community as you go to the local school, join the Scouts or the Little League, and follow one of the ways of life ac-cepted by your fellow-townspeople. But as you grow up, you have to make decisions as to whether you want to stay in this town or move elsewhere.

However, when adults move into a small town, they first make a conscious decision to do so. Then they have to go through a long process of finding out the town's story, of fitting into its ways, and of being accepted by those who already belong. And at various stages of their lives, they have to make further decisions as to how much they wish to be involved in the town's affairs and whether or not to stay or move away.

Similarly, there are two main ways of becoming an insider in the community of the Catholic Church. If you are born of parents who already belong to such a community, you are accepted as a member when you are a baby. In your early years, your parents and the community are responsible for teaching you its story and bringing you up in its ways. But gradually you have to take on responsibility for "growing up in Christ" as a member of this community. You have to make conscious decisions as to whether you intend to remain in it and how actively you will take part in its life.

But if, as an adult, you wanted to become a member of the Catholic Church, you would have to begin with a conscious decision to do so. This would be followed by a long process of becoming familiar with the Christian story and the way of life it calls for. Then you would be admitted as a full-fledged member.

So these two ways both initiate persons into the process of more and more complete "conversion" to the Lord's ways, to the life of the Spirit. But the sacramental celebrations of this initiation—Baptism, Confirmation, and the Eucharist—are held in a different order and with a different emphasis. There are, in fact, two different rites of baptism, for children and for adults, though the central expressive action is the same. This, as we all know, consists in immersing the person in water and/or pouring water over his or her head three times, while saying: "I baptize you in the Name of the Father . . . and of the Son . . . and of the Holy Spirit."

According to the present practice of our church community, the baptism of children is a brief celebration carried out, if possible, at a Sunday Mass so that the parish community can take part in it. The prayers and gestures which surround the central expressive action stress the children's being welcomed into the community and the community's responsibility—particularly that of the parents and godparents—to bring up the children as Christians.

Since baptized children belong to the church community, they have the right to take part in the Eucharist according to their ability and are allowed to receive Communion as soon as they know enough about the Christian story to realize that this bread and wine are a very special food and drink. And they are confirmed later on, with the same Rite as that used for adults, usually when they should be beginning to take some real responsibility for their own Christian development.

This is, obviously, the way in which most Catholics, in our country at least, are initiated into the church community. But the way in which adults are to be initiated shows much more clearly what the lifelong process of becoming more and more an insider demands and promises. And so it is considered the "norm" or standard way to be studied and reflected on.

Persons who have some real interest in becoming Catholic Christians, after a period of inquiry, are admitted to the "Order of Catechumens" in a brief ceremony expressing their intention and the community's welcome of them as potential members. They then go through a lengthy period of more thorough instruction in the story and the "ways of the Lord," and also come to know and be known by the local community. At the end of this period comes the Rite of Election in which they are enrolled as candidates for admission to the community. This is followed by a third period, one of intense spiritual preparation, preferably coinciding with Lent, which prepares the whole Christian community for the Easter celebration and renewal of its baptismal commitment. Then, during the Easter Vigil, the candidates are baptized, confirmed, and take part in the Eucharist for the first time, all in one grand celebration. Finally they are launched into Christian living by a period of deepened instruction during the Easter season.

In these essays, we have been reflecting on the story and how to live it. And we have already explored some of the wealth of meaning of the Eucharistic sign, the third of the "sacraments of initiation." We shall now consider, then, the central expressive actions of Baptism and Confirmation as signifying the process of becoming more and more insiders.

Plunged into Water

All of us can recognize the creative and recreative powers of water, both through our own experiences and through secondhand ones from films and TV shows, which we can remember and reflect on. How often after taking a shower or a bath, for instance, have you said something like, "I feel like a new person!"

It is easy to see, then, why, in the Bible, water is associated with the life-giving Spirit or "breath" of God. In the beginning, Genesis tells us, "the Spirit of God was moving over the waters" to make them life-giving. And through the prophet Joel, God promised to "pour out his Spirit on all flesh," as if the Spirit were water— a prophecy which St. Peter is recorded in Acts as seeing fulfilled in the coming of the Spirit on Pentecost.

But dirt has to be scrubbed and washed away before you can feel like "a new person"—not always a pleasant process. Small children usually delight in the feel of water: it's the cleaning part of washing that they object to.

In biblical thinking, dirtiness is a symbol of the sinfulness from which one must be cleansed before receiving the new life of the Spirit. For example, Psalm 51 prays: "Wash me thoroughly from my iniquity and cleanse me from my sin . . . Purge me with hyssop [a soapy plant] and I shall be clean; wash me and I shall be white as snow . . . Create in me a clean heart, and put a new and right spirit within me. Cast me not away from thy presence, and take not thy holy Spirit from me."

So in Jesus' time and culture, a rite of baptism —that is, of being "plunged into" water—had become an accepted sign of a change of heart, a conversion to God's ways. Nobody needed to have this meaning explained. St. Mark's gospel simply says: "John the baptizer appeared in the wilderness, preaching a baptism of repentance for the forgiveness of sins . . . And there went out to him all the people of the country of Judea and all the people of Jerusalem; and they were baptized by him in the Jordan, confessing their sins" (1:4-5). And John told them, "After me comes he who is mightier than I . . . I have baptized you with water, but he will baptize you with the Holy Spirit."

Jesus, of course, needed no conversion, yet he came to John with his sinful fellow-countrymen. "And when he came out of the water, immediately he saw the heavens opened and the Spirit descending on him like a dove; and a voice came from heaven: 'Thou art my beloved Son; with thee I am well pleased'" (10-11).

The baptismal washing with water, then, symbolizes both the cleansing from selfishness and all the other attitudes and habits which keep us from following the Lord's ways, and also the gift of the new life of the Spirit which enables us to follow those ways. So it is called a "Rebirth."

But the water of baptism also has an even

deeper symbolism. Water can be destructive as well as creative. People who live in places liable to floods know this all too well, and so do swimmers, and all those who sail the sea. To be plunged into water may be to experience a deathly struggle, if not death itself.

Jesus took this meaning of being plunged into water and applied it to his own struggle with suffering and death. When James and John wanted him to promise them the best seats in the Kingdom, he asked them: "Are you able to drink the cup that I drink, or to be baptized with the baptism with which I am to be baptized?" (Mark 10:38).

And so St. Paul tells us: "Do you not know that all of us who have been baptized into Jesus Christ were baptized into his death? We were buried therefore with him by baptism into death, so that as Christ was raised from the dead by the glory of the Father, we too might walk in newness of life. For if we have been united with him in a death like his, we shall certainly be united with him in a resurrection like his" (Rom. 6:3-5).

Thus Baptism signifies the kind of life Christians are to lead—"dying daily" to our selfishness and laziness and whatever else stops us from attaining greater fullness of life for ourselves and others . . . going through these dyings to the life of the Spirit with Christ, to the glory of the Father.

Anointed with the Spirit

But our reflections on Baptism need to be enriched by reflections on the expressive action of Confirmation. This consists in the bishop's making the sign of the cross with his thumb, which he has dipped in chrism, on the person's forehead, while he says: "Receive the seal of the Holy Spirit, the Gift of the Father."

For the central sign of Baptism, while it speaks about new life in the Spirit, stresses our passing-over to this new life with all the efforts and "dyings" involved. But the central sign of Confirmation speaks about the vitality and the attractiveness of this new life. (This is perhaps why some of the chrism—a mixture of olive oil and spices—used in Confirmation is poured into the baptismal font, and why, toward the end of the baptismal Rite, the sign of the cross is made with chrism on the head of the newly-baptized.) This chrism is blessed by bishops in a very special ceremony each Holy Thursday and is also used in the ordination of priests and in the consecration of bishops.

But the meaning of oil for Christians flows from the age-old uses of various kinds of oil for soothing, strengthening, and beautifying—uses which are still common today. To "anoint" may not sound like a familiar activity, but we are doing it to ourselves whenever we use hand cream, or an after-bath lotion, or Oil of Olay or any other of the innumerable compounds which people use to make themselves more supple, comfortable, and attractive.

In biblical times, olive oil was used for many kinds of healing, strengthening, and beautifying, as well as being an essential kind of food. To have plenty of grain, wine, and oil meant prosperity or richness. So to be anointed with oil on the head came to mean the conferring of special powers and the presence of the Spirit of God. Priests were anointed this way, and so were prophets and kings.

And when the Hebrew people had been conquered and exiled from their land, the LORD promised to send One who would finally make all things well and establish his Reign forever. This Promised One would be at once prophet, priest, and king, anointed with the Spirit. Speaking for this One, the prophet Isaiah says: "The Spirit of the LORD is upon me, because the LORD has anointed me to bring good tidings to the afflicted; he has sent me to bind up the broken-hearted, to proclaim liberty to the captives and the opening of the prison to those who are bound, to proclaim the acceptable year of the LORD, to comfort all that mourn" (61:1-2). St. Luke's gospel tells us that Jesus read this passage aloud in the synagogue at Nazareth, and added, "This day this scripture has been fulfilled in your hearing" (Luke 4:16-21).

After Jesus' death and glorification, his disciples realized that he was indeed this promised Anointed One—"Messiah" in Hebrew and "Christos" in Greek. Looking back on his ministry, they understood that the visible coming down of the Spirit on him at his baptism in the Jordan had been the sign of his anointing. And experiencing his risen presence and the outpouring of the Spirit whom he had promised to send from the Father, they realized that he had been established as "the source of eternal salvation to all who obey him" (Heb. 5:9). Since it was this Christ whom his followers preached, they came to be known as "Christians."

Our anointing with chrism at Confirmation, then, is the special sign of our being anointed or infused with the Spirit, who is now the Spirit of Jesus as well as "the Gift of the Father." We are thereby called and enabled to act as "prophets," "priests," and "kings." A prophet "speaks for" God. So we can speak for God's love by doing the kinds of things that Jesus did. In whatever little or big ways open to us, we can bring good tidings to the afflicted, bind up the broken-hearted, proclaim liberty to captives, set free those bound in prisons, and comfort those who mourn. A priest offers sacrifice. We can offer ourselves with Jesus' sacrifice, to the praise of the Father, in the sense explained in the previous essay on the Eucharist. And rulers exercise authority, which properly means "increasing." We can "rule" by developing our own gifts and by serving others in such a way as to help them develop their gifts.

Thus as Baptism celebrates our going with Jesus through death to the life of the Spirit as children of the Father, so Confirmation celebrates that life and what we are enabled to do if we try to "walk by the Spirit" (Gal. 5:16). But these two sacraments of initiation are incomplete as descriptive signs of Christian living without the Eucharist. This is one reason why they are celebrated, if possible, in the context of a Eucharistic celebration. For the Eucharist is, above all, the sign of the community into which we are to be more and more completely initiated: the community of children of the Father, "co-heirs with Christ" (Gal. 4:6-7), one in the Spirit—the community for which we were made.

Questions for Review:

1) How is the initiation of adults different from that of children?

2) Why is water thought of as having creative and re-creative powers?

3) How does the central sign of Confirmation differ in meaning from the central sign of Baptism?

4) What is the significance of the oil (chrism) used in Confirmation?

5) Our having been anointed with chrism in Confirmation is a special sign that we have received the Spirit and that we are called to act as "prophets," "priests," and "kings." How can we do this?

Questions for Discussion:

1) What might be some of the possible advantages and disadvantages of being a "cradle Catholic"? of entering the church as an adult?

2) In trying to live the Christian story in the years ahead, what are some of the difficulties you foresee?

3) What might be some of the ways in which you could prepare yourself and be helped by others to meet these difficulties?

3 Journal Suggestions

Each and every person is in the process either of becoming insiders or of quitting some group he or she belongs to. Both these processes are difficult because they force us either to redefine our self-images or to assert ourselves against the wishes and opinions of others. Suggestions for this chapter will afford you a means of evaluating your stance toward groups you belong to.

4 From Sacrament to Service

Creative and intellectual involvement in the life of the church requires a conscious decision on our part. One way to begin is to look at the many options for service to the church community, and to the human community, which exist in the parish of which we are members. As one learns more about the structure of the parish, one can appreciate the many kinds of Kingdom-building work that are being done and can choose an area and a level of involvement.

The following activities are designed to help you understand your parish better and to see what kinds of services are given through your parish. The questions at the end of the section may help you decide how to become intelligently and creatively involved in renewal in your parish.

Form a group with other students who belong to your parish and then *choose one of the following activities* to research and to prepare a report for the class.

1) Make a list of all the persons who are involved in *full-time ministry* in your parish. Make appointments to interview them, and then write a description of their work and their concerns about the parish and its growth.

2) List those who are involved in *part-time ministry* in your parish. Make appointments to interview them and then be able to describe their work. How do they find time for this part-time ministry? Why is it important to them?

3) Learn more about the structure of your parish. Make appointments with your pastor, the associate pastor, the permanent deacon, and a member of the board of trustees. What are their major responsibilities? In what specific ways do they think the parish is being renewed?

4) Make a list of groups that are active in your parish. What service does each of the groups perform? Are there any special efforts being made in your parish to reach out to families, to single people, to the widowed, the shut-in, the elderly, to those in public schools, to the very young, to adults who want to continue their education and faith formation, to young people your age?

5) Describe some persons who minister to others in individual ways.

6) To gain a better understanding of the changes that are happening in the church, talk with one of your grandparents or another elderly parishioner about the things they find changed in the church today. Which changes are most difficult for them? Why? Do you think some of the things they miss about how the church "used to be" should have been kept?

As a class: Share the information you have gathered about the parishes of which you are members. Is there a great variety among them? Is there some unity evident in the variety? Do the parishes seem to be cooperating with one another to build God's Kingdom here on earth?

As a young person: Do you see yourself as an active member of your parish? Can you find a way to use your gifts to serve others through your parish—ways which will help carry out the church's mission to spread God's word to all the world and thus build up the Kingdom?

5 Para-Liturgy

Theme:

"I believe . . ."

Opening Song:

"If the Lord Does Not Build" by the St. Louis Jesuits.

Pray Together:

Today, Lord, I want to ask you to help me grow closer to you.

Reading:

A reading from the Good News according to Mark.
John the baptizer appeared in the wilderness, preaching a baptism of repentance for the forgiveness of sins. And there went out to him all the country of Judea, and all the people of Jerusalem; and they were baptized by him in the river Jordan, confessing their sins. Now John was clothed with camel's hair, and had a leather girdle around his waist, and ate locusts and wild honey. And he preached, saying, "After me comes he who is mightier than I, the thong of whose sandals I am not worthy to stoop down and untie. I have baptized you with water; but he will baptize you with the Holy Spirit."
In those days Jesus came from Nazareth of Galilee and was baptized by John in the Jordan. And when he came up out of the water, immediately he saw the heavens opened and the Spirit descending upon him like a dove; and a voice came from heaven, "Thou art my beloved Son; with thee I am well pleased" (1:4-11).

Response:

Let us proclaim our faith by saying together the Creed.

Ritual:

Let us recall what we use water for in our daily lives: to clean, to wash, to drink. Jesus used water as a symbol of cleaning and as a sign of new life. As the leader pours the water over your hands, he/she will say the following words: "I cleanse your hands and invite you to become more like Christ." Your response is "Amen."

Response:

Right Side: Many are invited but few say "Yes."

Left Side: Lord, help me become more of a believer.

Right Side: Many say "Yes" in words but through their dealings with other people say "No."

Left Side: Lord, help me become more of a believer.

Right Side: Many become unbelievers when times get rough.

Left Side: Lord, help me become more of a believer.

(Additional prayers may be added.)

Shared Prayer:

The Christ-Candle is a symbol of Jesus as light of the world. I invite each of you to hold the candle in your hand and, if you choose, to say a prayer out loud.

Pray Together:

Lord, help us to be people who day-by-day continue to grow in our love and faith in you. Help us, Lord, to live our faith and not just talk about it. Amen.

Closing Song:

"You Have Been Baptized in Christ" by Rev. Carey Landry.

Anointing of the Sick and Penance:
Celebrations of Healing and At-One-ing

Chapter 7

1 Orientation

How often do we learn about something by learning what it is not? Even such obviously good things as the Christian story and community are not as well-grounded in our lives as we would like to think. Often the story goes untold. People stop treating each other as the sons and daughters of God, as brothers and sisters of Jesus. And all too often a prison of some kind replaces community.

Even in our daily lives, we experience once in a while a feeling of being shut off from friends and family. Perhaps it happens because we make someone suffer. Or perhaps we are the victim of an insult or an embarrassment. In any case, when we lose the affection or encouragement of others, we begin to doubt ourselves and to feel lonely. It is not the aloneness of hiding out with an exciting novel or of a long hot bath on a cold day. Rather, it is the feeling of being for the moment with someone we don't quite like or trust—ourselves. Elder Olson found an imaginative way of describing this feeling in his poem "Directions to the Armorer":

All right, armorer,
Make me a sword—
Not too sharp,
A bit hard to draw,
And of cardboard, preferably.
On second thought, stick
An eraser on the handle.
Somehow I always
Clobber the wrong guy.

Make me a shield with
Easy-to-change
Insignia. I'm often
A little vague
As to which side I'm on,
What battle I'm in.
And listen, make it
A trifle flimsy,
Not too hard to pierce.
I'm not absolutely sure
I want to win.

Make the armor itself
As tough as possible,
But on a reverse
Principle: don't
Worry about its

Saving my hide;
Just fix it to give me
Some sort of protection—
Any sort of protection—
From a possible enemy
Inside.

As imprisoned as we seem to be in our loneliness, it is marvelous how these prison bars evaporate before someone's caring smile. And we find that a friend's kindness or a parent's affection can clothe us in something better than armor—a kind of aura of well-being. When this occurs, we sense in ourselves the need for community. We begin our search for others who share that need. Consequently our friendships deepen.

The essay which follows deals with our imprisonment in wrongdoing and in suffering, and with the sacraments which celebrate the Kingdom-building works of forgiveness and healing. Before you begin reading it, think for a moment about the kinds of armor or defenses you feel you need to wear. Does anyone you know live in a kind of prison?

2 Reading and Discussion

Celebrations of Healing and At-One-ing

My mother-in-law once made what has become a classic statement in our family, to be used on all appropriate occasions. She had suffered a mild stroke, and when she regained consciousness, my husband asked her how she felt. She whispered, "I feel bad, and I don't *like* to feel bad."

We have all experienced many kinds of "feel-ing bad" and realized that we didn't like them at all—even if we were trained not to admit it. We have "felt bad" physically, from a sprained ankle or a burn, or the stuffy misery of a bad cold, or the fever and itching of chicken pox. We have also "felt bad" emotionally from being embarrassed or snubbed or afraid.

What makes all these kinds of "feeling bad"

worse is the sense they bring with them of being cut off from other people, enclosed in our own misery. When we have deliberately hurt someone, we obviously cut ourselves off from him or her and also from the community that we both belong to. Illness and severe pain make us feel isolated in a different way, cut off from the life and activities of healthy people.

The Christian story does not give us a clear explanation of why God allows so much and so many kinds of "feeling bad." It does, however, suggest that a great deal of suffering is the effect of the inhumanity of man to man—something borne out by psychology, sociology, and the other behavioral sciences.

Humankind has thus woven, generation after generation, a very tangled web of sin and suffering into which we are all born and by which we are influenced. Many forces inside and outside us, for which we are not responsible, tend to keep us imprisoned in our own self-interest and acting in ways that add to this web of misery and misdoing. These forces make up what has traditionally been called "original sin." They are ways, not to life, but to death—death of people's humanity as well as physical death.

But God wants to free us from our imprisonment in our own self-interest. He wants us to help one another, in his Spirit, towards the fullness of life Jesus came to make possible for us, rather than diminishing others' lives or destroying them. Since Jesus has gone through death to fullness of life, and so made death a way to life, we no longer need to be afraid of the "daily dyings" we may have to undergo. We can enter willingly into the process of "dying to" our selfish selves and living by the Spirit, the process described by the sign of Baptism.

Moreover, in Jesus, God has experienced human suffering from within. And even though Jesus is now fully living the glorious life of the Kingdom, in him God somehow still suffers in and with all who suffer. So we can believe, though we cannot understand it, that somehow suffering can have worth and meaning.

Yet God's will is for our healing, our "wholeing" ("heal" and "health" and "whole" and "holy" all come from the same root). And this must finally mean the healing and the whole-ing of groups and societies as well as individuals. God does not want us passively to accept others' suffering. He does not want us to accept our own sinfulness, or that of the social structures in which we are involved. He wants us to be healed and to heal, to be reconciled and to reconcile.

When we take part in the Eucharist, we celebrate these remedial aspects of the work of preparing for the Kingdom as well as celebrating all its other aspects. We celebrate everything that people have done, are doing, and will do, in the Spirit of Jesus, to carry out his work of healing and whole-ing persons and societies, and we commit ourselves afresh to that work.

But since wrongdoing and suffering are such evident realities in our lives and in our world, the church provides special sacramental signs of God's healing and forgiving love: the Anointing of the Sick and Reconciliation of Penitents. These are not only signs of the Christian community's concern for its sick and its sinful members but celebrations of all kingdom-preparing works of healing and reconciling.

The Anointing of the Sick

We naturally tend to avoid thinking about the possibility of serious illness for ourselves and those close to us. Yet it is obviously sensible to know at least when to call what doctor or hospital and what the procedure is likely to be in dealing with one or another form of illness. So also Catholics ought to know when it is appropriate to ask for the Anointing of the Sick, from the parish priest if the patient is at home or from hospital or nursing-home chaplains.

Any Catholic who is seriously ill from sickness or old age may receive this Anointing, and "seriously" is to be broadly interpreted. For example, the directives say that "old persons may be anointed if they are in weak condition although no dangerous illness is present."

These directives go on to say: "In public and private catechesis, the faithful should be encouraged to ask for the anointing and, as soon as the time for anointing comes, to receive it with complete faith and devotion, not misusing this sacrament by putting it off. All who care for the sick should be taught the meaning and purpose of anointing."

The Anointing is not, of course, meant to be a substitute for medical care. It is directed to the healing of persons on all levels of their being—"body, mind, and soul," as the blessing for the oil puts it. Physical cures, even dramatic ones, have followed it, and we should always be open to this possibility. But only God knows what kinds of healing will best promote the total well-being of a particular sick person. Many pilgrims to Lourdes, for instance, have returned home with the physical ailments they went with. But they report feeling healed in other ways that made all the effort more than worthwhile. And so it is with the healings to be expected from Anointing.

The central expression of this sacrament is, as we all know, the anointing of sick persons on the forehead and hands with oil by an appointed representative of Christ and the Christian community. The oil is first blessed with a prayer that "all who are anointed with this oil may be freed from pain and illness, and made well in body, mind, and soul." While the priest is anointing the sick person he says, "Through this holy anointing may the Lord in his love and mercy help you with the grace of the Holy Spirit. Amen. May the Lord who frees you from sin save you and raise you up. Amen."

Here, as in Confirmation, oil tells us something about the Spirit. You know how good it feels when you put a soothing lotion on your badly chapped hands, or spread a healing ointment on a sore and itchy cut. So the Spirit is the "Comforter," which means consoler and strengthener.

We should also mention another expressive action common to Confirmation and the Anointing of the Sick, and also Orders: the "laying on of hands" before the Anointing. We all know how encouraging and comforting an affectionate touch can be whether it takes the form of a slap on the back when we have accomplished something, or a cool hand on our forehead when we are feverish. The "laying on of hands," then, is a ritualized form of such gestures, communicating strength and power—hence, the healing and strengthening power of the Spirit of Jesus.

Rites of Reconciliation

Most of us were brought up on the "going to Confession" form of the Sacrament of Penance. This form seemed to many people at least, to have the pattern of an impersonal judicial proceeding, with the penitent the accused—even though self-accused—and the confessor the judge, who ascertained the degree of guilt present and assigned an appropriate penalty before "wiping the slate clean."

The "Rites for the Reconciliation of Penitents," however, seem modeled rather on the parable of the Prodigal Son, with the father running out to welcome the repentant wastrel before he had a chance to begin his confession and giving orders at once for a feast to celebrate the son's return. The change in tone, as

well as in form, invites us to take a new look at this sacrament, to see why and when we might want to take part in it.

As we saw earlier, the process of becoming more and more completely insiders in God's community of love involves turning away from our own ways, our own self-centeredness, to follow God's ways. But this is not a turning-around, or conversion, which can be accomplished once for all. With the power of the Spirit, we have to free ourselves gradually from attitudes and inclinations that tend to pull us back "outside."

It is possible to turn away completely from God and his ways, as if one made a complete U-turn on a highway. This is called "mortal" sin, from the Latin word for "death," since it means deliberately choosing the death of self-centeredness and of alienation from God and other people. Most authorities today believe that people who are generally trying to follow God's way would be most unlikely suddenly to make such a drastic change of life-direction. We are more likely to turn aside, so to speak, from God's way and take another road, not completely in the wrong direction, but more or less so. And we are very likely, because of original sin, as described above, to discover that we have been on a wrong road without intending or realizing it.

When we do realize that we have hurt other people, if possible, we go to them and say we are sorry and want to make up. Then we need to have them give us some sign of forgiveness and reconciliation, which means "coming together again."

Now God is involved in this whole process. We have turned away from his love in acting unlovingly. We have added to Jesus' sufferings, since he suffers in the suffering we cause ourselves and others. It is his Spirit that enables us to turn back to love. And it is also his Spirit that enables those we have harmed to forgive us. God does indeed forgive us as soon as we turn back to love. But just as we need some sign of other people's forgiveness, so we need some sign of God's forgiveness, of being again "at one," or more "at one," with him. (We need such a sign all the more, perhaps, in situations when it isn't possible to ask forgiveness directly of people we have harmed and to make up quickly with them—for example, if you have been looking down on and making life difficult for a group of your fellow students.) And such a sign can only be given us by a person whom we believe to have the power to "speak for" God. We have also harmed the whole community of those who are working with Jesus, in the Spirit, for the Kingdom, since, to a greater or lesser extent, we have hindered rather than cooperated in this work. And so we need some sign of the community's forgiveness, of being "at one" with it again—a sign which can only be given by an appointed representative of this community.

The full sacramental sign of the forgiveness of

God and of the people of God is, of course, the sacrament of Penance, carried out through one or another of the Rites for the Reconciliation of Penitents. But these are signs, not only of this forgiveness but also of the whole process of any reconversion, or deeper conversion, to the Lord's ways, and so they can increase our understanding of and commitment to that process.

If you go to a confessor as an individual penitent, you should have your choice of an anonymous situation with a screen between you and the priest or a more personal, face-to-face setting. In either case the priest, representing Christ and the church, takes the initiative. As the directives for this Rite put it, he "should welcome the penitent with fraternal charity and, if the occasion permits, address him with friendly words." Thus the Rite begins with this sign of God's love "reaching out" to help us repent and be reconciled.

Then the priest and the penitent make the sign of the cross, acknowledging their faith in the presence of God the Father, Son, and Spirit and in Jesus' victory over sin through his death and resurrection. Next the priest briefly urges the penitent to have confidence in God, preferably using a brief sentence from Scripture, and encourages him or her to read or repeat from memory some other appropriate brief scriptural passage.

Next, the penitent confesses his/her sins, which might include, not only specific actions but also unloving tendencies or attitudes, perhaps only recently recognized as such. One does not need to try to express everything one sees to be wrong with oneself and one's actions. For this confession is essentially a sign of admission of sinfulness and our need for God's Spirit to enable us to act lovingly. The priest offers counsel, as seems to be indicated, and imposes a "penance"—an act of prayer or self-denial or service—a sign of the wider effort called for to make up for having harmed the work of Kingdom-building, and a sign of the intent to engage in it more wholeheartedly. The penitent manifests his contrition and resolution to begin a new life by means of a prayer for God's pardon. It is desirable that this prayer should be based on words of Scripture.

Following this prayer, the priest extends his hands, or at least his right hand, over the head of the penitent [a laying on of hands] and pronounces the formula of absolution, in which the essential words are: "I absolve you from your sins in the name of the Father and of the Son and of the Holy Spirit." As he says the final words, the priest makes the sign of the cross over the penitent.

The Rite then concludes with a brief "celebration" in which the penitent praises God's mercy with some short passage taken from Scripture, and the priest tells him to go in peace.

The Sacrament of Penance is, then, meant to be a very rich sign of God's merciful love enabling us again and again to turn more directly and wholeheartedly to his ways than we have been doing, or to turn back to them when we have gone seriously astray.

You might, therefore, want to avail yourself of this sacrament when you feel discouraged and confused, or just generally "a mess," as well as when you have done some specifically and deeply unloving action. You might even want to do so simply to help you realize afresh that God's Spirit is at work in our world, enabling people to repent of wrongdoing and to try to make up for it and enabling people to forgive those who have wronged them.

Questions for Review:

1) What are some of the ways that "feeling bad" cuts us off from other people?

2) What are some examples given in the essay to show how suffering is caused by the inhuman ways people treat other people?

3) Why is it a misuse of the Sacrament of the Anointing of the Sick to put off receiving it, or put off seeing that a sick person has an opportunity to receive it?

4) The use of blessed oil and the "laying on of hands" are two expressive actions used in the Anointing of the Sick; how are they reminders of the healing power of the sacrament?

Questions for Discussion:

1) How would you describe a healthy Christian attitude towards one's own physical sufferings? towards those of others?

2) What values might there be in taking on some form of voluntary discomfort or inconvenience—e.g., not eating meat on certain days of the week, giving up candy during Lent . . . ?

3) We aren't personally responsible for the long-standing injustices perpetrated by our society, such as the treatment of native Americans throughout U.S. history. Many people, consequently, say that they don't feel any responsibility for righting these wrongs and making up for them. How would you answer such a statement?

3 Journal Suggestions

When we suffer at the hands of someone else or when we ourselves hurt someone, we carry memories as scars of the experience. We must then heal these memories in ourselves and help to heal others. One way to do this is to describe the hurt, in much the same way that a certain tennis coach has players draw a circle around the hurt place and locate the pain on a scale of one to ten. The Journal Suggestions for this chapter afford you an opportunity to begin this process of healing by getting in touch with the pain.

4 From Sacrament to Service

The essay spoke about the web of injustice into which we are born and which influences our behavior. As a result, in many situations, we have to make decisions about the possible rightness of doing what seem to be unjust actions. The following activity may help you understand more clearly the difficulty of making decisions in such situations, the necessity of making some decision, and the range of decisions possible.

1) Around the room are six signs with the following headings:

Against 100%	Against 80%	Against 60%
For 60%	For 80%	For 100%

2) When a situation is read to you and you are asked to respond, take a position in one of the six areas of the room according to your own beliefs, values, and attitudes toward the situation. For example, if you are in 100% agreement with the situation, move to the "For-100%" area. If you are mostly in agreement, but have some reservations, move to the area marked "For-80%."

3) There is no 50-50 position. You must make a choice and cannot remain neutral.

4) Be ready to explain why you took the position you did. What are your strong reasons for being where you are? What are some reservations you have?

Situation 1: You are a B+ student and have been working at a job after school to earn money for personal needs and to pay your tuition. Because of your long hours of work lately your schoolwork has been suffering and you are not prepared for the big test coming up. You have the opportunity during the test the next day to copy from a friend of yours who sits next to you in class. You know that you would have been prepared for the class if you had not had to work so many extra hours, so you go ahead and copy from your friend so you can keep your B+ average in the class.

Situation 2: You are a part-time worker in a large department store. Because you are only part-time, you are not paid as much as full-time workers who are doing exactly the same work you are doing. When the opportunity arises, you shoplift small items. You justify this by thinking that the store is so large the manager will never miss the small items you take, and besides, they "owe" it to you because you are unjustly underpaid for your work.

5 Para-Liturgy

Theme:

To start fresh again

Opening Song:

"Brother Jesus" by Rev. Carey Landry.

Opening Prayer:

I have fallen, Lord, once more. I can't go on, I'll never succeed. I am ashamed, I don't dare look at you. Lord, I knew you were right near me, bending over me, watching. All I had to do was call. But temptation blew like a hurricane, and instead of looking at you, I turned my head away. There you stood silent and sorrowful. There I stood, alone, ashamed, and disgusted. You loved me and I forgot you. But you said: Come, look up. Isn't it your pride that is wounded? If you loved me, you would not grieve, but you would trust. Do you think that there is a limit to God's love? Do you think for a moment that I stopped loving you? But you still rely on yourself. You must rely on me. Ask my pardon and get up quickly. You see, it's not falling that is the worst, but staying on the ground.
All: Amen.

Reading:

Let us listen now to God's word as he speaks to us about sharing and being for others. A reading from the prophet Isaiah.
"This is the fasting that I wish, that you refrain from controlling others; that you work for others' freedom; that you love others enough so they can experience being themselves; that you share your food with the hungry; that you generously give aid and hospitality to those in need; that you willingly respond to the cry of others for help especially those in your own family. Then, when you do these things, your light will shine forth, and your own pains will quickly be healed."

Response:

Leader: Having heard God's word with open hearts, let us now express our sorrow for our failings.
Right Side: For the times we have doubted your love and mercy . . .
Left Side: We are sorry, Lord.
Right Side: For our weaknesses and laziness in turning to you in prayer . . .
Left Side: We are sorry, Lord.
Right Side: For our indifference and apathy we show toward our fellow human persons . . .
Left Side: We are sorry, Lord.
Right Side: For our lack of reverence for the gift of life in all its forms.
Left Side: We are sorry, Lord.

Ritual:

Oil is a sign of strength and healing. The leader will come to each of you, place some oil on your forehead in the sign of the cross, and will say: "May the God of love and peace heal you and make you one with him again." Your response is "Amen."

Closing Prayer (or Spontaneous Prayer):

God, we love you and one another. We are sorry for the times that we hurt one another and you, for the times we have failed to help one another. Help us to be more loving in words and in actions. Fill us with your spirit of peace and healing. Amen.

Closing Song:

"Peace Is Flowing like a River" by Rev. Carey Landry.

Persons and Communities as Sacraments

Chapter 8

1 Orientation

Saying No

People learn to say no at a very early age. Every parent has had amusing—if not exasperating—mealtime conversations with a two-year-old. A typical exchange might go something like this:

"Will you please eat your cauliflower?"

"No."

"Don't you like your cauliflower?"

"No."

"Will you eat your hot dog?"

"No."

"At least eat your hot dog."

"No."

"How about your ice cream bar?"

"No."

Of course the ice cream bar question is a tip-off that the real issue is not food. Left alone, the child will tend to finish whatever is on the plate. The child actually says no to assert his self or her self against the wishes of the parent. This kind of "no" is vital to the child's growth because it indicates that the child recognizes himself or herself as a person independent of the parent.

As we grow up, however, saying no becomes a more difficult task. For one thing we have more and more relationships to handle. And our relationships become much more complicated than the one-sided, parent-and-child kind. Further, we begin to join groups or at least become more active members of groups we belong to.

It reaches the point sometimes when it seems that practically everyone around us wants something of our time or efforts or thinks they know what we should be doing better than we do. For instance, parents expect us to help out, to be home at an early hour, to do homework, and generally to see things *their* way—that is, to be moral and to achieve. Our friends, on the other hand, demand that we are available at any hour, that we treat school as a joke, and generally that we see things *their* way—that is, to be spontaneous and aloof. And that is not the end of it. TV pours out thousands of messages about how to "come alive" in our culture. At the same time, rock songs and rock heroes suggest all kinds of counter-culture styles.

Choosing to whom or what to say no can become exhausting. More than that, at times it becomes nerve-racking because some people won't take no for an answer. It is hard to keep telling a friend no and downright dangerous to say no to a group of friends. Furthermore, you can't respond to a silly TV ad or a foolish song lyric. In fact, saying no has become difficult for so many people today that there are best-selling books

and countless workshops every year which teach self-assertion by re-teaching people how to say no.

On the whole, saying no takes a grim and sometimes agonizing effort on our part. But it is always to good purpose when it flows from our need to grow, rather than just to change, from our sense of integrity rather than an urge to lose ourselves, from our concern to protect our unique talents and insights and values rather than to pretend that we are no different than anyone else. The poet Robert Frost once wrote that "fences make good neighbors." Saying no is our attempt to build the kinds of fences between ourselves and others that make us worthwhile neighbors—or sons or daughters or friends.

Saying Yes

The tip-off question in the conversation with the two-year-old suggests that we must also learn when to say yes. And there are many things in our lives we should say yes to—besides ice cream bars. In fact, we can't exist very happily just refusing and rejecting any more than we can enjoy letting others decide what we will do with our lives. Obviously we must decide what *we* want from life.

The following essay deals with lifestyles and with living as sacraments ourselves. Before reading it, try to imagine filling your life with an activity to which you can say yes continuously and as joyously as C. S. Lewis felt when he once wrote: "If one could run without getting tired, I don't think one would often want to do anything else." As you read the essay, try to imagine which life-style might afford you the best opportunity to say yes to your life interests.

2 Reading and Discussion

Persons and Communities as Sacraments

These essays have tried to describe what sacramental celebrations have to do with our daily living. To take fruitful part in a liturgy, we must come together as a community of believers in the Lordship of Jesus, and his presence with us, believers who are trying—however imperfectly—to act on our belief. Together we hear about some ways in which the Christian story gives meaning and value to our lives. We represent the story in a symbolic action, praise God for it, and take joy in it. In so doing, we anticipate the final future of the story, the Kingdom come. We also see more clearly the ways in which we are to prepare for the Kingdom, and gain courage and hope to follow these ways.

Moreover, as Christians we are not only called, together with everyone "who loves and practices justice," to prepare for the Kingdom. We are also called to proclaim it as God's loving design for creation. We are called to tell the Christian story and to do so above all by our attitudes and actions. We are called to be living signs or sacraments of God's love as shown and given to us in Jesus.

And we are called to try to be sacraments in this sense not only as persons but also as communities of persons. The Good News we have to proclaim is precisely that God wants and intends to draw persons into community of life and love with him and with one another and with all creation. Consequently, communities and a community of communities are needed to be signs of this community-in-the-making and of how we are to prepare for it.

In this chapter, then, we shall briefly explore some of the implications of this sacramental vocation for Christian persons and communities and also, in this context, the special sign-values of the traditional states of life: single life, Religious life, marriage, and the priesthood. Finally, in the following chapter we shall consider our responsibilities towards the church itself as a sacrament.

To say that we are called to be sacraments of God's love to all our neighbors, near and far, certainly does not imply that we are continually to be worrying about our "image" in the Madison Avenue sense. It means simply that we are to try to carry out the great commandments to love God and neighbor after the example of Jesus, by cultivating the attitudes and lines of action described and celebrated in the seven sacraments. As the three previous chapters indicated, the Anointing of the Sick and Penance shows us our call to be healers and reconcilers; Baptism and Confirmation, our call to try to free people *from* dehumanizing forces and to free them *for* life in abundance with God and one another. Above all, the celebration of the Eucharist shows us our call to give and share life, even at the cost of laying down our own lives.

We can, of course, find opportunities for cultivating these attitudes and carrying out these lines of action whatever our circumstances. And taking advantage of the opportunities available to us, however seemingly insignificant, can be a preparation for future work on a wider scale and concerned with some crucial issue. For example, learning to be patient with and really helpful to a trying elderly relative might be one kind of training for community organizing to improve its quality of life in some essential area.

But, obviously, some life-styles—in the sense of the use of time and energy and things—are more conducive than others to "walking in the Lord's ways." People who are trying to keep up with the Joneses as pictured in TV ads, by acquiring houses, cars, clothes, gadgets, and so on, are unlikely to be able to spend much effort on promoting caring and sharing, justice and peace, even on their own family level.

Life-style in the sense of use of time and energy and things obviously cannot be separated from life-style in the sense of various kinds of relationships with other people. And these are necessarily deeply conditioned by our attitudes toward, and our use of, our own sexuality and that of others. We are called to love one another "in deed and in truth" (1 John 3:18), and to do so as sexed persons, men and women. And this means that we are to try, however slowly and painfully, to bring our sexuality into the service of this kind of loving, rather than of self-centeredness.

The scope of these essays does not permit an exploration of this most vital aspect of our sacramental vocation. But it should be clear from what has already been said that we are called to try, with the help of the Spirit, to make all our ways of loving and expressing love become healing and whole-ing ways, freeing and community-building ways, life-giving and life-sharing ways —for ourselves and for those we love.

All Christians, then, share a common vocation to become more and more effective signs of the Christian story and to help one another do so in communities which, as communities, are trying to carry out this same vocation. This might seem an impossible assignment. Yet all of us know some persons and even, perhaps, some groups who do indeed give us a sense of God's gracious presence and action.

Of course, the efforts of individuals and communities vary widely with personalities, circumstances, and opportunities, and the unchartable

gifts of the Spirit. But, as you are looking ahead to what God may call you to become and to do, it might be useful to consider very briefly the particular contribution to Christian witnessing associated with the four traditional states of life.

Single Life

Until fairly recently, neither society nor the church considered the single life as a desirable state except for persons too young to make a permanent commitment to one of the other states. In fact, in Catholic parlance, for a long time only persons who entered the priesthood or the "religious life" were said to have vocations— that is, a positive call to grow in the love of God and neighbor and to serve the Kingdom. Even though it is one of the seven sacraments of the Catholic Church, it was only in the 1930's and '40's that marriage began to be considered as a vocation in this sense. But now that the vocation of all Christians is once again being emphasized, it is becoming clear that leading a single life, whether temporarily or permanently, is also a "calling."

There are, of course, many different kinds of singleness—of young people and older people, widowed or divorced. But the kind that will personally concern you for the next few years is that of the uncommitted young adult. And it is most important that you do not feel that this stage in your life is a kind of marking time until you "settle down" in marriage or some other form of permanent commitment. In fact, the particular value of this kind of singleness flows from its comparative freedom to discover and develop one's gifts, to search out and try out different life-styles, with all the mistakes and difficulties involved. Persons in this "seeking" state of life might, then, serve as signs to other members of the Christian community of the pilgrim character of the Christian life, its basic unsettledness in the world as it is.

But this pilgrimage is not meant to be a lonely one. Christian persons living in any kind of singleness have a need and a right to be fully included in the life and activities, the caring and sharing of Christian communities, such as parishes. And the more they do so, as both givers and receivers, the more these communities will be signs that we are all one in Christ, whatever our human status.

Religious Life

The term "Religious," in this usage, simply means "living by a rule" (from the Latin *religare,* meaning "to bind"). Many different forms of Religious life have been developed through the ages, some more devoted to prayer, some to action. What they have in common is a commitment, permanent or temporary, to follow a rule of life designed to facilitate growth in the love of God and neighbor and service of the Kingdom. This commitment includes celibacy chosen for the freedom it should provide to serve the Kingdom and to give witness to the reality of God's love, in and beyond all human loves. Moreover, except for the rare vocation to a hermit's life, it includes commitment to a community of persons following the same rule and trying to make their communal life a sign of the perfect loving community of the Kingdom.

Religious communities today are re-examining their rules and their actual life-styles in order more effectively to give their particular witness. And it is one very much needed by the church and by our society. The possibility of becoming a mature "whole" person without sexual intercourse is one which our world needs to see realized in actual living persons in order to find it believable. And all kinds of people are looking for workable models of "community." Young people would do well, then, to become acquainted with some of the varieties of the Religious life as it is being lived today. At the least, this would be one way of broadening one's ideas as to the potentialities of Christian community living, some of which might be adapted to other kinds of communities.

Married Life

The sign-value of married life is already suggested in the Bible. The Hebrew Scriptures speak frequently of the covenant relationship between the Lord and his people in terms of a marriage, and St. Paul speaks of the "profound mystery" of marriage as related to Christ and the church (Eph. 6:21-35). In the times when they were written down, these interpretations upgraded marriage and the status of women. For in those cultures, a woman was legally the property of her husband, and arranging a marriage was a matter of business rather than affection. To see marriage as establishing a covenant relationship of love, then, was a recognition of women as persons, not things. (Scripture scholars say that this is also the bearing of the account of the creation of Eve in Genesis 2:19-25).

But today these interpretations seem clearly not to do justice to St. Paul's less culture-conditioned insight that "there is neither male nor female, for you are all one in Christ Jesus" (Gal. 3:28). It would be preferable, then, to see married life as meant to be a sign of the faithful love of God for human persons, the love which the Spirit pours out in our hearts, enabling us faithfully to love God and one another.

Thus, when a man and woman enter into a sacramental marriage, they should realize that their exchange of vows is meant to signify their commitment to try to make their life together such a sign of God's faithful love. (The operative word here is "try"—no one can promise to be successful.) But, in fact, all of us know some couples and some families who, in spite of difficulties and mistakes and confusion, do convey the sense that creative fidelity to love is possible, that trying lovingly to share life is worth doing. Such families are "open circles," radiating warmth and inviting others to share it. They are needed by single persons, priests, religious, or lay, and by other families; they are needed by their communities. And they need the faithful and caring love of their communities. The family community cannot do without the wider community, and vice versa.

Orders

"Holy Orders is one of the seven sacraments recognized by the Church; it consecrates and enables a baptized Christian to fulfill the functions of a bishop, priest or deacon." Such a definition does not imply a state of life in the same sense as those we have just discussed. And, indeed, in the present discipline of the Roman Catholic Church, married men may become permanent deacons. Priests and bishops must be celibate, and they may belong to Religious communities. And much discussion is being carried on as to whether they might not also have the option of marriage (and whether the "baptized Christian" in the above definition might not be a woman).

Nevertheless, Catholic people generally expect some special witness from those "in" Orders, and rightly so. But we need to realize that this witness is meant to remind us of some particular aspects of our own vocation and not simply to be admired in others.

The particular witness, or sign-value, of the Order of Deacon is clear from the term itself: "deacon" means "server." And so those who are deacons are meant, through their work and life-style, to be signs of the vocation of the whole church and all its members to "serve the men of the modern world ever more generously and effectively."

In chapter 6, we noted that our anointing with chrism at Confirmation is a sign of our calling to act as "prophets," "priests," and "kings." Similarly, priests are anointed with chrism at their ordination, and bishops at their consecration, as a sign of their vocation to live and act in such a way as to remind their fellow-Christians of their own prophetic, priestly and kingly calling and to help them carry it out.

Thus all these "states of life" are complementary. None of them can do without the others if we are to form one Body working through its many members to be a sign and servant of the Kingdom.

Questions for Review:

1) What does it mean to say that we are called to be "sacraments" of God's love to all our neighbors near and far?

2) Describe the "calls" we have received through the sacraments discussed in chapters 5, 6, and 7.

3) What is the common vocation shared by all Christians?

4) What are some of the particular values of the single life?

Questions for Discussion:

1) What are some of the essential elements of any Christian life-style or state of life?

2) Read St. Matthew's gospel, 6:24-33, and 2 Thess. 3:6-13. What do these passages, taken together, imply about the main thrust of truly Christian life-styles and states of life?

3) Do you think that it would be a good idea if, in your parish and neighborhood, people of different ages and states in life had more opportunities to do things together?

3 Journal Suggestions

2000 A.D. What will the world look like in the next century? Will our lives be drastically different than now or amazingly the same? Probably both.

The Journal Suggestions for this chapter will afford you an opportunity to speculate about your own future.

4 From Sacrament to Service

We are living in an age of much transition, choice, and variety of options when it comes to choosing a life-style. Along with the variety of options come the questions: What does it mean to be committed to someone or to something? Why is it that today, people are waiting until they are older to choose a life-style? Is it because of the variety of options? Is it because they want to take time to make the right choice? Is fear part of their reason for not deciding till later in life—fear about "will my marriage, life as a religious, a priest, last only a few years?" What does it really mean to say "yes" to someone in a relationship or friendship? What does it really mean to volunteer to give service or to choose one's life-style?

Throughout both the Old and the New Testament, God speaks of "faithfulness" in the relationship between himself and his people. The Hebrew word *hesed* is translated as "steadfast love." If we agree with the idea of a total willingness to love and to serve our God and his people, and agree that each of us is invited into this relationship, then how can we make the best possible choice to love and serve our God and his people?

Jean Smith, in her book *Take More Joy*, raises some important aspects of what it means to make the right choice and to be faithful to one's choice or commitment:

Finding one's way in the world could be compared to walking along a road

or path. Sometimes the way is straight, other times it curves and climbs. One walks on steppingstones or crosses bridges. Sometimes one walks with another person or with several others. Frequently, one walks alone. Under any circumstances, the walk through life is a personal journey, for each must find his own way and come to the realization of who he is and where he is going.

The following activities will help you understand better how people "find their way" in the world. Choose one of the activities and plan a way to share your interview with the class.

Activity One: Spend some time talking with a young person who is making decisions about life-style and life-work. (Someone just beginning college with plans to enter a particular career; someone just joining one of the armed forces; someone beginning a new job; a young person about to be married, or ordained, or entering Religious life.) What helped them reach their decision? What are their expectations? special joys? deep concerns? What makes them sure they made the right choice, or aren't they sure?

Activity Two: Talk with someone older who seems to have made a successful choice of life-style and life-work. Why have they stayed married to the same person for so many years? Or why have they never married? Or why have they remained in the priesthood or religious life? Why have they been content with the job they have held for so many years? Have their hopes and expectations been fulfilled? If they had another chance, would they make the same choices?

5 Para-Liturgy

Theme:

Called to share our "gifted-ness" with God's people

Opening Song:

"Take, Lord, Receive," by the St. Louis Jesuits.

Pray Together:

Lord, you have invited each of us from birth to follow you and to be people who spread your word. Regardless of what life style we choose, our goal is to grow closer to you, God, and to share your word and love with your people. Amen.

First Reading:

Finding one's way in the world
    could be compared to walking
    along a road or path.
Sometimes the way is straight;
    other times it curves and climbs.
    One walks on s-t-e-p-p-i-n-g
        s-t-o-n-e-s
        or crosses bridges.
Sometimes one walks with
another person or
with several others.
    Frequently, one walks alone.

Under any circumstances,
the walk through life is a personal journey,
for each must find his own way and come to the
realization of who he is and where he is going.

Ritual Sign:

As a sign of Christ's personal invitation to serve his people, each person is invited to light his/her candle from the Christ-Candle and hold it. While this is taking place, the following song could be played: "Wherever You Go," by Monks of Weston Priory.

Second Reading:

A reading from the prophet Jeremiah 1:5-8. "'Before I formed you in the womb I knew you, and before you were born I consecrated you; I appointed you a prophet to the nations.' Then I said, 'Ah, Lord God! Behold, I do not know how to speak, for I am only a youth.' But the Lord said to me, 'Do not say, "I am only a youth"; for to all to whom I send you you shall go, and whatever I command you you shall speak. Be not afraid of them, for I am with you to deliver you, says the Lord.'"

Response:

Right Side: Lord, you invite each of us as Christians to serve your people.

Left Side: Help us, Lord, to serve and be served.

Right Side: Lord, you invite each of us to love all people regardless of race, faith, physical deformities, or age.

Left Side: Help us, Lord, to serve and be served.

Right Side: Lord, you invite each of us to follow you.

Left Side: Help us, Lord, to serve and be served.

(Additional prayers may be added at this time.)

Sharing of My Gift:

Take a moment to think about a gift you have which you could share with someone else.

Closing Prayer:

Read the "Desiderata."

Closing Song:

"Where You Would Not Go" by Followers of the Way.

The Church as Sacrament

Chapter 9

1 Orientation

Someone once said that we should all live our lives led by our visions rather than pushed by our problems. The idea makes immediate sense to us since no one likes being pushed into anything, let alone by our problems. Further, the thought of being guided by our visions is attractive, for great leaders and great thinkers live this way. The psychoanalyst Carl Jung, for instance, wrote in his autobiography: "All my works, all my creative activity, have come from those initial fantasies and dreams which began in 1912, almost fifty years ago. Everything I accomplished in later life was already contained in them, although at first in the form of emotions and images." As another example, the vision St. Paul had of Jesus on the road to Damascus redirected his life's work from that of persecuting the early Christians to becoming their foremost advocate and missionary.

Visions are often the result of much serious thinking upon some subject, even on a somewhat unconscious level. Jung, for instance, used a journal to pursue an intense self-study, recording his dreams and fantasies. A more extreme case would be the prolonged meditation and praying by the young men of certain American Indian tribes in conditions of isolation and near-starvation.

Visions can be kept private, quietly filling a person's existence with meaning, or they can be shared. For instance, while Jung spent his life studying his visions, St. Paul shared his in preaching. Again, while Indians often kept their visions very secret, poets and artists, on the other hand, need to express their visions to us. And because visions are often in the form of images, people talk about them using imagery. Consider, for example, the following poem by Richard Brautigan entitled "All Watched Over by Machines of Loving Grace":

> I like to think (and
> the sooner the better!)
> of a cybernetic meadow
> where mammals and computers
> live together in mutually
> programming harmony
> like pure water
> touching clear sky.

> I like to think
>   (right now, please!)
> of a cybernetic forest
> filled with pines and electronics
> where deer stroll peacefully
> past computers
> as if they were flowers
> with spinning blossoms.

> I like to think
>   (it has to be!)
> of a cybernetic ecology
> where we are free of our labors
> and joined back to nature,
> returned to our mammal
> brothers and sisters,
> and all watched over
> by machines of loving grace.

Until we get used to it, this poem seems strange and comic. The images are dreamlike. These are qualities it shares with many other visions along with two important elements. First, it joins together things which ordinarily clash in life or at least in our thinking. So the vision provides, if only in images, an ultimate solution to an apparent dilemma. Second, this poem, like many visions, is open-ended, leaving open the way to God. Here Brautigan recognizes that his paradise could be regulated by machines only if they possessed "loving grace." Brautigan's vision, then, affords us an insight along with a clearly religious hope.

The essay which follows discusses St. Paul's hopeful vision for the church which he describes as the body of Jesus, "ascended far above all heavens, so that he might fill the universe." Before you read the essay, try to imagine the church as you would see it in its ideal form. How does your idea relate to the discussions of community in the previous chapters?

2 Reading and Discussion

The Church as Sacrament

The previous chapter suggested the interdependence of persons and communities in carrying out the Christian vocation. It should be obvious, then, that just as we each have a part in "making" sacramental celebrations, so we each have a part to take in helping the Christian communities to which we belong become more effective sacraments of God's love.

This is true of our membership in any kind of community gathered together in Jesus' name. We all know, for instance, how one member of a family, or a class, or a small group, can be a peace-maker or a peace-destroyer. But the idea that "ordinary" laypeople have any responsibility towards their church—beyond contributing money—is a new one to most Catholics although it is clearly the New Testament ideal. And so this is the aspect of Christian community that we shall discuss in this final essay.

For centuries Catholics generally have been convinced that the well-being and mission of their church is solely the concern of the Pope, bishops, and priests. These were said to constitute "the teaching church," while the laity were the passive "learning church." Consequently, laypeople who took on any church-related responsibilities were said to be "sharing in the work of the hierarchy," rather than taking part in the life and work of the church as first-class members.

But then, only a few years ago, the Second Vatican Council proposed a return to the New Testament ideal. Obviously, to implement this return in actual practice is necessarily a long and painful process; age-old ways of thinking and acting, and the structures which these have formed and been formed by, are not easily

changed. If you keep trying to live and celebrate the Christian story as a member of the Roman Catholic Church, you will necessarily be involved in this process. And if you are to be intelligently and creatively involved, you need some estimate of the situation. You need some picture of the ideal, of what happened to it in the course of history, and what efforts are now being made to return to it and try to approach it.

The background of this picture, and a background we should never lose sight of, is the fact that the church and church communities are made up of imperfect people—people like ourselves. Consequently they are subject to all the problems of any human community, even though their members are gathered together in Jesus' name and by his Spirit. It has always been this way, and we have no right to expect that it will be otherwise until the Kingdom fully comes.

The Acts of the Apostles tells us that the three thousand persons converted by Peter's preaching on the first Pentecost "devoted themselves to the apostles' teaching and fellowship, to the breaking of bread [that is, the Eucharist] and the prayers . . . and all who believed were together and had all things in common" (2:42ff). But the situation soon became less ideal: "Now in those days, when the disciples were increasing in number, the Hellenists murmured against the Hebrews because their widows were neglected in the daily distribution [of food]" (6:1). St. Paul's Letters certainly make it clear that the churches he established were not always models of peaceful caring and sharing. Yet he continued tirelessly to describe what they should be, urging them to "lead a life worthy of the calling to which you have been called, with all lowliness and meekness, with patience, forbearing one another in love, eager to maintain the unity of the Spirit in the bond of peace" (Eph. 4:1-2).

So it has been down through the ages and is today. The whole church and the local churches which embody it, as well as the individual members, continually fall short of their calling. But the Spirit of Jesus continues to raise up persons to remind them of that calling and its demands. Thus the Second Vatican Council, in its document on the church, describes it as a "pilgrim" community, one that has not yet achieved its ideals, "given strength to show forth in the world the mystery of the Lord in a faithful but shadowed way."

Consequently, we may be disheartened, but we should not be disillusioned to find a church community carrying out its vocation as we ourselves carry out ours—in a way that may often seem more shadowed than faithful. That is why the whole church and each of its local communities, as well as each of its members, are called to "repent and be converted." This is why "renewal" is always needed.

The many-sided renewal proposed by the Second Vatican Council includes, as was mentioned earlier, a reaffirmation of the idea presented in many ways in the New Testament: All the members of the church together are "the church" and are called to be "a holy priesthood" (1 Peter 2:5), and each has a particular contribution to make to its life and mission. St. Paul uses the image of a living body several times to describe this idea and its implications. Animated by the one Spirit, this body has Christ as its head, "from whom the whole body, joined and knit together by every joint with which it is supplied, when each part is working properly, makes bodily growth and builds itself up in love" (Eph. 4:10).

Or again, "for as in one body we have many members, and all the members do not have the same function, so we, though many, are one body of Christ, and individually members of one another. Having gifts that differ according to the grace given to us, let us use them . . ." (Rom. 12:4-6).

Or again, "for just as the body is one and has many members, and all the members of the body, though many, are one body, so it is with Christ. For by one Spirit we were all baptized into one body . . . and were made to drink of one Spirit. For the body does not consist of one member, but of many. If the foot should say, 'Because I am not a hand I do not belong to the body,' that would not make it any less a part of the body. And if the ear should say, 'Because I am not an eye I do not belong to the body,' that would not make it any less a part of the body. If the whole body were an eye, where would be the hearing? If the whole body were an ear, where would be the sense of smell? But, as it is, God arranged the organs in the body, each of them, as he chose . . . As it is, there are many parts, yet one body. The eye cannot say to the hand, 'I have no need of you,' nor again the head to the feet, 'I have no need of you.' On the contrary, the parts of the body which seem to be weaker are indispensable . . . God has so composed the body, giving greater honor to the inferior part, that there may be no discord in the body. but that the members may have the same care for one another. If one member suffers, all suffer together; if one member is honored all rejoice together. Now you are the body of Christ and individually members of it" (1 Cor. 12:12-27).

St. Paul is saying, as strongly as he can, that Christ's church is not meant to be characterized by uniformity or conformity, but by unity in variety: "varieties of gifts, but the same spirit . . . varieties of service, but the same Lord;

and varieties of working, but the same God who inspires them all in every one. To each is given the manifestation of the Spirit for the common good" (1 Cor. 12:4-7). The church community, then, isn't meant to be made up of rulers and ruled, or teachers and taught, but of persons with different gifts serving one another and carrying out the church's mission together.

However, as many people who have tried to found communes have painfully discovered, every enduring community has to have a center. Some person(s) have to be responsible for seeing to it that what is essential to the community's life and work gets done, ensuring both unity and continuity.

The Early Church and the Church Today

As we saw above, the apostles began to form a community of believers on the first Pentecost, a community of which they collectively were the center. But soon they found that they needed help in preserving its unity. So they asked the whole "body of disciples" to choose wise men, full of the Spirit, to be what we now call deacons, meaning "servers." By a laying on of hands they empowered—or as we would say, "ordained"— those chosen.

Then, as the apostles separately began to establish Christian communities or "churches" in different places and moved on to establish new ones, they empowered men chosen by each community to be its center: to preside over the Eucharist, see that the Gospel was rightly proclaimed, keep in touch with other churches, help the members of their community serve one another in love, and ordain successors to this office.

Various other ministries seem to have been recognized in these early churches. St. Paul mentions "first apostles, second prophets, third teachers, then workers of miracles, then healers, administrators, speakers in various tongues" (1 Cor. 12:28). But the central, coordinating ministry was that just described, a ministry handed on from an apostle. Those who exercised it at first seem to have been called either *episcopi*, bishops, or *presbyteroi*, priests. In later developments, the office of bishop came to be considered the central ministry in each church but was carried out in close association with a group of priests and deacons.

Then, when a local church gained so many members that all could not conveniently celebrate the Eucharist together, the bishop deputed one of these priests to celebrate it in his stead for a certain section of the community. And so our present parish system began to develop, with each parish forming a community within the wider community of what we call a "diocese," and the dioceses and particular groups of dioceses all together making up the church.

Ideally, this structure could be that of a community of communities, with unity-in-variety among them, as among the members of each local "church." This unity would then be personally signified by the Pope, who is the Bishop of Rome and so is the successor of St. Peter.

However, in the history of the Roman Catholic Church, due to many kinds of cultural and other forces, this structure came to seem less and less like a community of communities, and more and more like a pyramid—with the Pope as its apex, then bishops, then priests, then the laity, all in separate layers, with a sharp dividing-line between clergy and laity, and communication coming only from the top down. Obviously, this image has very little in common with St. Paul's description of a living body in which every cell and organ has its function or with what the first letter of Peter says about all the members of the church forming a "royal priesthood" (1 Peter 2:4).

At the same time, it became more and more a monarchical structure, with the Pope ruling the whole, the bishops and their priests and laypeople, and pastors the "flocks" entrusted to them by their bishops. This style of leadership hardly seems in keeping with Jesus' teaching: "You know that those who are supposed to rule over the Gentiles lord it over them, and their great men exercise authority over them. But it shall not be so among you; but whoever would be great among you must be your servant, and whoever would be first among you must be slave of all. For the Son of Man came not to be served but to serve" (Mark 10:42-44). In practice, certainly, innumerable bishops and priests have and do serve their communities humbly and lovingly, but the accepted style of exercising authority hardly made it easier to do so.

Renewing such pyramidal church communities and the whole Catholic Church in accordance with the image of a living body, actively serving the Kingdom, is, obviously, a most challenging enterprise and one that is taking many forms. For example, laypeople are being appointed to more or less official ministries in the celebration and life of their parishes—as lectors, extraordinary ministers of communion, directors of religious education, catechists.

But what is most important in this many-sided work of renewal is that we all—whatever our age, our "state in life," our particular circumstances and gifts—are being urged to take whatever means may be most helpful to "grow up in every way into him who is the head, into Christ" (Eph. 4:15), and so serve the Kingdom. And this is the effort which, as these essays have tried to show, the sacraments both signify and celebrate.

Questions for Review:

1) What part do laypeople have in the New Testament ideal of the church as a Christian community?

2) How can you explain that the whole church (the local churches and their members) is in need of renewal?

3) Explain how St. Paul describes the fact that all members of the church are "the church" and how each has a special contribution to make to the life and mission of the church.

4) Why does every enduring community need to have a person or group of persons as its center?

Questions for Discussion:

1) What does "the Church" mean to you in terms of a picture? of persons?

2) Someone once wrote that we don't find it very difficult to live with our own faults and failings, but we do find it extremely difficult to live with those of other people. Do you think that it is particularly difficult to stand the faults and failings of persons officially associated with our church? If so, why?

3) What are some of the ways in which persons serve the church and the Kingdom apart from recognized "ministries" and church organizations?

3 Journal Suggestions

The suggestions for this chapter will give you some ideas of what your journal might become for you. Continue journal-making on your own. Adapt the techniques you used in earlier chapters to suit your purposes. Remember: you have nothing to lose and everything to gain from the time you spend journal-making.

4 From Sacrament to Service

Pope Paul VI in his encyclical "On the Development of Peoples" said that all people need "freedom from misery, the greater assurance of finding subsistence, health and fixed employment; an increased share of responsibility without oppression of any kind and in security from situations that do violence to their dignity as men; better education—in brief, to seek to do more, know more and have more in order to be more . . ."

Take some time to read carefully and reflect on the following "Bill of Rights." Select one of the rights and prepare a report which describes an example of a person or a group of persons who have taken specific action to preserve or defend that right or who have helped some person or group benefit from that right.

Make your report factual and show how the person or group helped others to have a better quality of life. Your example may be taken from the national scene, from your city or town; you may also look for persons in your school (teachers, students, staff) and among your parents and other adults in your parish or neighborhood.

You might find it helpful to jot down ideas that came to your mind as you read the "Bill of Rights." Are there some people you want to talk with about their work for freedom, some magazine or newspaper articles you remember reading that might help you with this report? Perhaps you have seen a documentary on television which dealt with someone's efforts to insure one of these freedoms.

Can you think of some direct action you, your friends, or your class could take which would help someone have one of these rights?

A Bill of Rights

1) **The Right to Life**
   Freedom of the unborn from abortion and the aged from euthanasia

2) **The Right to Peace and to Respect for one's Person and Property**
   Freedom from war and violence

3) **The Right to a Pure and Clean Earth and the Protection of Health**
   Freedom from polluted streams and air and freedom from disease

4) **The Right to Adequate Food, Clothing, Decent and Open Housing**
   Freedom from poverty and life in the ghetto

5) **The Right to Education**
   Freedom from ignorance and inferior and defective education

6) **The Right to Employment**
   Freedom from discrimination in hiring and in obtaining training

7) **The Right to Privacy**
   Freedom from wiretapping, from secretly compiled personal files, and from the indiscriminate divulging of personal information

8) **The Right to Information and Truth**
   Freedom from deceit, from being kept uninformed and ignorant by government and other public bodies

9) **The Right to Due Process of Law and Equal and Impartial Enforcement of Law and Administration of Justice**
   Freedom from harassment and from double legal standards

10) **The Right to Children and Family**
   Freedom from legislation limiting or repressing the rights of parents to bear and educate children

5 Closing Prayer

Creating Our Christian Community

Opening Song:

"Take My Hand" by Monks of Weston Priory.

Pray Together:

Father, help us to follow in your Son's footsteps creating the Christian Community in our day. May we carry on the building and realize that all things are possible with and in you. Amen.

First Reading:

A reading from Paul's first letter to the Corinthians.

For just as the body is one and has many members, and all the members of the body, though many, are one body, so it is with Christ. For by one Spirit we were all baptized into one body—Jews or Greeks, slaves or free—and all were made to drink of one Spirit.

For the body does not consist of one member but of many. If the foot should say, "Because I am not a hand, I do not belong to the body," that would not make it any less a part of the body. And if the ear should say, "Because I am not an eye, I do not belong to the body," that would not make it any less a part of the body. If the whole body were an eye, where would be the hearing? If the whole body were an ear, where would be the sense of smell? But as it is, God arranged the organs in the body, each one of them, as he chose. If all were a single organ, where would the body be? As it is, there are many parts, yet one body. The eye cannot say to the hand, "I have no need of you," nor again the head to the feet, "I have no need of you." On the contrary, the parts of the body which seem to be weaker are indispensable, and those parts of the body which we think less honorable we invest with the greater honor, and our unpresentable parts are treated with greater modesty, which our more presentable parts do not require. But God has so composed the body, giving the greater honor to the inferior part, that there may be no discord in the body, but that the members may have the same care for one another. If one member suffers, all suffer together; if one member is honored, all rejoice together. Now you are the body of Christ and individually members of it (12:12-27).

Response:

Right Side: Lord, help us to be generous with our time and talents, willing to share them with our community.

Left Side: Lord, help us to prepare for the Kingdom.

Right Side: Lord help us to speak out when we see things that need to be improved in our community.

Left Side: Lord, help us to prepare for the Kingdom.

Right Side: Lord, help us become vital members of our community.

Left Side: Lord, help us to prepare for the Kingdom.

(Additional prayers may be added at this time.)

Second Reading:

A reading from the Good News according to Matthew.

Narrator: A man who was going on a journey calls together his laborers. He gives one person five talents, to another two talents, and to a third one talent.

Crowd: What should I do with my talent?

Narrator: The person with five talents went out and traded them and had five more talents.

Crowd: What should I do with my talent?

Narrator: The person with two talents did the same.

Crowd: What should I do with my talent?

Narrator: The person who had one talent dug a hole and hid it.

Crowd: What should I do with my talent?

Reflection:

How will you use your talents? Will you share them with the community? or save them?

Closing Prayer:

Lord, help me to become a person willing to share my talents with the community to the best of my ability. Amen.

Closing Song:

"Trust in the Lord" by the St. Louis Jesuits.